200 SCHOOL SCIENCE EXPERIMENTS

DR DHEERAJ MEHROTRA

Contents

Preface

Welcome to the world of hands-on exploration and discovery! ***"200 School Science Experiments"*** *is a treasure trove of engaging and educational experiments designed to captivate students' curiosity and inspire a love for science. This collection has been carefully curated to provide teachers, educators, and young scientists with diverse experiments that make learning enjoyable and impactful.*

Science is not merely a subject to be studied; it is a dynamic and thrilling journey into the mysteries of the world around us. The experiments within this book are crafted to foster a sense of wonder, encouraging students to ask questions, make predictions, and actively participate in the scientific method. From biology to physics, chemistry to astronomy, these experiments cover a broad spectrum of scientific disciplines, ensuring a comprehensive and enriching experience for learners of all ages.

As we delve into the pages of this book, we embark on a voyage of exploration, where the classroom transforms into a laboratory of possibilities. Each experiment is designed with simplicity and safety in mind, making them accessible for educators with varying levels of resources and expertise. The goal is to teach scientific concepts and instil critical thinking skills, a spirit of inquiry, and a passion for lifelong learning.

This collection is a testament to the belief that science is best learned by doing. Through hands-on experimentation, students understand scientific principles and experience the joy of discovery. The experiments are structured to encourage collaboration, communication, and a sense of accomplishment as young minds unravel the intricacies of the natural world.

I am grateful to the educators, scientists, and enthusiasts who have contributed to this compilation. Your dedication to inspiring the next generation of scientists is evident in the creativity and thoughtfulness embedded in each experiment. May this book spark curiosity, ignite a passion for science, and nurture the budding scientists in our classrooms.

So, let the experiments begin! Here's to a journey of exploration, learning, and celebrating the endless wonders science offers.

Happy experimenting!

Dheeraj Mehrotra

Author

CHAPTER ONE

IMPORTANCE OF SCIENCE EXPERIMENTS IN SCHOOLS

Experiments in the scientific method are integral to a well-rounded education because of their many advantages. The following reasons best show the significance of scientific experiments in the classroom:

Practical Experience:

Science experiments allow students to engage in active learning via hands-on activities. They may better understand and retain scientific ideas when participating in hands-on activities.

Putting Academic Understanding to Use:

Between classroom theory and its practical implementation, experiments provide the missing link. Students may deepen their comprehension of the subject by seeing the application of scientific ideas in real-world scenarios.

Abilities in Critical Thinking:

Experiment design and execution foster analytical reasoning. The process of issue analysis, hypothesis development, and conclusion drawing helps students develop a scientific worldview and strong problem-solving abilities.

Wonderment and Questioning:

Children learn by doing, and experiments are a great way to foster their natural curiosity. Students acquire an authentic curiosity about *the world and understand the value of inquiry by going beyond what is taught in the classroom to investigate real-world issues.*

Improved Holding Power:

Taking part in experiments helps you remember more of what you learn. Students' memorization and comprehension of course content improve when they actively participate in their education.

The Real-World Implications of Scientific Procedures:

Students learn the scientific method via experiments, a systematic way to investigate a topic by observing, making hypotheses, conducting experiments, analyzing data, and drawing conclusions.

Working together as a team:

Student cooperation is essential for many experiments. Interpersonal competence, clear expression of ideas, and the capacity to pool resources for analysis are all enhanced by teamwork.

Improvement of Abilities:

A wide variety of abilities, such as working with scientific equipment, conducting accurate measurements, analyzing data, and conducting tests, are honed by participation in scientific investigations. A wide range of scientific disciplines may benefit from these hands-on abilities.

The Development of an Appassion for Science:

An optimistic outlook on science may be fostered via interactive and pleasurable activities. The material becomes more meaningful to students when they see its application in their everyday lives.

Get Ready for Real-Life Obstacles:

The problem-solving procedures one encounters in real life are similar to those reflected in experimentation. Students acquire marketable abilities that may be used in a wide range of professional contexts, as well as in scientific inquiry and technological progress.

Hope for the Next Generation of Scientists:

Scientific, technological, engineering, and mathematics (STEM) occupations may be a source of inspiration for children when they do experiments. Engaging in hands-on activities early may spark an interest in science.

Being able to change and adapt:

Responding to unexpected findings or changing protocols is a standard part of scientific investigations. The dynamic nature of scientific inquiry necessitates this development in its practitioners.

To sum up, scientific experiments provide a dynamic and engaging way to learn and are essential to the educational process. Students' personal growth and establishment of a lasting love of science are aided by developing their critical thinking, practical skills, and natural curiosity fostered via experimentation.

CHAPTER TWO

EXPERIMENTS

NOTE: To Teachers/ Instructors/ Parents:

Ensure that these experiments are conducted in a safe and supervised environment. Adjust the complexity and details based on the grade level and available resources.

Volcano Eruption:

Materials: Baking soda, vinegar, dish soap, modelling clay.

Create a model volcano and simulate an eruption by combining baking soda and vinegar.

~

Dancing Raisins:

Materials: Clear soda, raisins.

Drop raisins into a glass of soda and observe the dancing motion caused by carbon dioxide bubbles.

~

Balloon Inflation with Vinegar and Baking Soda:

Materials: Balloon, vinegar, baking soda.

Create a chemical reaction by combining vinegar and baking soda inside a balloon.

~

Rainbow in a Jar:

Materials: Sugar, water, food colouring.

Layer different concentrations of sugar water to create a colourful gradient.

Density Tower:

Materials: Various liquids (water, oil, syrup) and small objects.

Explore density by layering liquids of different densities in a transparent container.

Magnetic Slime:

Materials: Liquid starch, glue, iron filings, magnet.

Create slime with magnetic properties by adding iron filings.

Oobleck:

Materials: Cornstarch, water, food colouring.

Explore the properties of non-Newtonian fluids by mixing cornstarch and water.

Static Electricity Butterfly:

Materials: Paper, scissors, static electricity source (e.g., a charged balloon).

Create a butterfly that moves with the power of static electricity.

Bending Water with Static Electricity:

Materials: Balloon, water, a small stream of water.

Generate static electricity and observe its effect on a stream of water.

Egg in a Bottle:

Materials: Hard-boiled egg, bottle, matches.

Demonstrate air pressure by placing a peeled, hard-boiled egg on a bottle.

Lemon Battery:

Materials: Lemon, copper and zinc electrodes, LED.

Generate electricity by creating a simple lemon battery.

Germination Experiment:

Materials: Seeds, soil, containers.

Investigate the factors affecting seed germination under different conditions.

Cabbage pH Indicator:

Materials: Red cabbage, water, various household substances.

Create a pH indicator using red cabbage and test the acidity of different substances.

Surface Tension Experiment:

Materials: Water, dish soap, pepper.

Explore surface tension by placing pepper on water and observing its reaction to soap.

Solar Oven:

Materials: Cardboard box, aluminium foil, plastic wrap.

Build a solar oven and observe its ability to cook food using sunlight.

Milk and Soap Experiment:

Materials: Milk, food colouring, dish soap.

Observe the reaction between milk, food colouring, and soap to create colourful patterns.

Glowing Water:

Materials: Tonic water, blacklight.

Discover the fluorescent properties of tonic water under UV light.

Colour-Changing Carnations:

Materials: White carnations, water, food colouring.

Observe how plants absorb water by placing white carnations in the coloured water.

DIY Lava Lamp:

Materials: Oil, water, food colouring, effervescent tablets.

Create a homemade lava lamp combining oil, water, and effervescent tablets.

Baking Soda and Vinegar Rocket:

Materials: Film canister, baking soda, vinegar.

Create a simple chemical reaction to launch a film canister into the air.

Mentos and Soda Geyser:

Materials: Mentos candies, soda.

Create a spectacular geyser by dropping Mentos candies into a bottle of soda.

Chromatography Butterfly:

Materials: Coffee filters, markers, water.

Explore chromatography by creating colourful butterflies using water and markers.

Homemade Electromagnet:

Materials: Iron nail, copper wire, battery.

Build an electromagnet by wrapping copper wire around an iron nail and connecting it to a battery.

Exploding Baggies:

Materials: Baking soda, vinegar, sealable plastic bag.

Produce a gas-filled reaction in a sealed baggie with baking soda and vinegar.

~

Tornado in a Jar:

Materials: Jar, water, dish soap.

Simulate a tornado by swirling water and dish soap in a jar.

~

Rain in a Jar:

Materials: Jar, shaving cream, food colouring.

Depict the concept of precipitation by creating "rain" in a jar using shaving cream and food colouring.

Invisible Ink:

Materials: Lemon juice, paper, heat source.

Write secret messages using lemon juice and reveal them with heat.

Egg Drop Experiment:

Materials: Eggs, various packaging materials.

Design and test different packaging materials to protect an egg from a fall.

Static Electricity Bell:

Materials: Balloon, aluminium pie tin, string.

Create a static electricity bell by charging a balloon and attracting it to an aluminium pie tin.

~

Colour-Changing Milk:

Materials: Milk, dish soap, food colouring.

Observe the interaction between fat molecules in milk and soap, resulting in colourful patterns.

Disappearing Eggshell:

Materials: Egg, vinegar.

Investigate the reaction between eggshells and vinegar, which dissolves the shell.

Homemade Thermometer:

Materials: Plastic bottle, straw, water, clay.

Construct a simple thermometer to measure temperature changes.

DIY Rainbow Density Column:

Materials: Various liquids with different densities, clear container.

Layer liquids to create a colourful density column, showcasing the principle of density.

Balloon-powered Car:

Materials: Balloons, plastic bottles, wheels.

Build a balloon-powered car to explore the principles of air pressure.

DIY Cartesian Diver:

Materials: Plastic bottle, water, eye dropper.

Create a Cartesian diver to demonstrate the effects of pressure and buoyancy.

DIY Barometer:

Materials: Glass jar, balloon, rubber band.

Construct a barometer to measure atmospheric pressure changes.

Bouncing Egg:

Materials: Vinegar, egg.

Explore the concept of osmosis by submerging an egg in vinegar, resulting in a bouncy texture.

DIY Electroscope:

Materials: Aluminum foil, plastic straw, small pieces of paper.

Build a simple electroscope to detect static electricity.

Sugar Crystal Growing:

Materials: Sugar, water, string, pencil.

Grow sugar crystals on a string to observe crystallization.

Homemade Stethoscope:

Materials: Funnel, tubing, balloon.

Create a simple stethoscope to explore sound transmission.

DIY Cartesian Diver:

Materials: Plastic bottle, water, eye dropper.

Create a Cartesian diver to demonstrate the effects of pressure and buoyancy.

Water Cycle in a Bag:

Materials: Ziplock bag, water, blue food colouring, tape.

Observe the water cycle by creating a miniature model in a sealed bag.

DIY Lava Lamp:

Materials: Oil, water, food colouring, effervescent tablets.

Create a homemade lava lamp combining oil, water, and effervescent tablets.

Colourful Celery Experiment:

Materials: Celery stalk, food colouring, water.

Investigate how plants absorb water by placing celery in the coloured water.

DIY Sundial:

Materials: Cardboard, pencil, compass.

Build a simple sundial to understand how the sun's position affects shadows.

DIY Periscope:

Materials: Cardboard, mirrors, tape.

Construct a periscope to explore the reflection of light.

Density of Liquids:

Materials: Various liquids and small objects.

Experiment with the density of liquids by observing the floating or sinking of objects.

Homemade Gluep:

Materials: Borax, glue, water, food colouring.

Create a non-Newtonian fluid known as "gluep" by combining borax and glue.

DIY Wind Vane:

Materials: Straw, paper, pencil, compass.

Build a wind vane to determine the direction of the wind.

Magnetic Maze:

Materials: Magnet, paper clips, cardboard.

Create a magnetic maze to explore the principles of magnetism.

DIY Cloud in a Jar:

Materials: Jar, hot water, ice, hairspray.

Simulate the formation of clouds by creating condensation in a jar.

Chromatography Flowers:

Materials: Coffee filters, markers, water.

Explore chromatography by creating colourful flowers using water and markers.

Homemade Rock Candy:

Materials: Sugar, water, string, pencil.

Grow edible rock candy crystals by dissolving sugar in water.

Walking Water Experiment:

Materials: Paper towels, water, food colouring.

Demonstrate capillary action by observing water move between paper towels.

DIY Kaleidoscope:

Materials: Cardboard tube, coloured beads, reflective paper.

Create a kaleidoscope to explore the reflection and symmetry of light.

Tin Foil Boat Challenge:

Materials: Tin foil, water basin.

Design and test tin foil boats to understand buoyancy and water displacement.

DIY pH Indicator:

Materials: Red cabbage, water, various household substances.

Create a natural pH indicator using red cabbage to test the acidity of substances.

Homemade Bouncy Balls:

Materials: Borax, glue, cornstarch, water.

Craft bouncy balls by combining household ingredients.

DIY Solar Still:

Materials: Plastic wrap, container, sunlight.

Create a solar still to observe the process of water evaporation and condensation.

Rubber Egg Experiment:

Materials: Vinegar, egg.

Investigate the effects of acid on eggshells by submerging an egg in vinegar.

DIY Microscope Slide:

Materials: Water dropper, transparent slide, small specimen.

Create a simple microscope slide to observe small specimens under magnification.

DIY Hovercraft:

Materials: CD, balloon, bottle cap.

Build a hovercraft to explore the principles of air pressure and motion.

Color-Changing Milk Experiment:

Materials: Milk, dish soap, food colouring.

Observe the reaction between fat molecules in milk and soap, resulting in colourful patterns.

~

DIY Cartesian Diver 2.0:

Materials: Plastic bottle, straw, clay.

Create an improved Cartesian diver using a straw and clay.

~

DIY Tornado Tube:

Materials: Two plastic bottles, water.

Construct a tornado tube to simulate a vortex in a bottle.

~

Homemade pH Scale:

Materials: Red cabbage and various household substances.

Create a homemade pH scale using a red cabbage indicator.

DIY Solar Water Heater:

Materials: Aluminum foil, plastic bottle, water.

Build a simple solar water heater to understand solar energy absorption.

~

Egg Osmosis Experiment:

Materials: Eggs, vinegar, water.

Investigate osmosis by submerging eggs in vinegar and observing changes.

~

DIY Rainbow Fizzing Tablets:

Materials: Baking soda, citric acid, food colouring.

Create rainbow fizzing tablets to explore chemical reactions.

~

Balloon Rocket Experiment:

Materials: String, straw, balloon.

Construct a balloon-powered rocket to study the principles of thrust and propulsion.

DIY Potato Battery:

Materials: Potato, zinc and copper electrodes, wires.

Build a potato battery to generate electricity.

DIY Invisible Ink with Lemon Juice:

Materials: Lemon juice, paper, heat source.

Write invisible messages using lemon juice and reveal them with heat.

Candle Water Rising Experiment:

Materials: Candle, water, glass jar.

Observe water rising inside a jar as a candle burns.

DIY Fireworks in a Jar:

Materials: Oil, water, food colouring, effervescent tablets.

Create a visual display resembling fireworks in a jar.

Walking Rainbow Experiment:

Materials: Water, cups, food colouring, paper towels.

Explore capillary action by creating a walking rainbow.

DIY Seed Germination Test:

Materials: Seeds, wet paper towels, plastic bags.

Conduct a seed germination test to observe plant growth.

DIY Spectroscope:

Materials: Cardboard, CD, scissors.

Construct a simple spectroscope to observe light spectra.

Egg Geode Crystals:

Materials: Eggshells, alum, water, food colouring.

Grow crystal geodes inside empty eggshells.

DIY Cartesian Diver 3.0:

Materials: Plastic bottle, eyedropper, water.

Enhance the Cartesian diver experiment with an eyedropper.

DIY Fog in a Bottle:

Materials: Warm water, ice, plastic bottle.

Create fog in a bottle to understand the concept of condensation.

DIY Homopolar Motor:

Materials: Battery, copper wire, neodymium magnet.

Build a simple homopolar motor to demonstrate electromagnetic principles.

DIY Magnetic Slime:

Materials: Liquid starch, glue, iron filings, magnet.

Create slime with magnetic properties by adding iron filings.

DIY Crystal Snowflakes:

Materials: Borax, pipe cleaners, hot water.

Grow crystal snowflakes using the process of crystallization.

DIY Rainbow Density Tower:

Materials: Various liquids, clear container.

Layer liquids of different densities to create a colourful density tower.

DIY Cartesian Diver 4.0:

Materials: Plastic bottle, straw, small plastic container, water.

Explore buoyancy with an advanced Cartesian diver using a small container.

DIY Fire Snake:

Materials: Baking soda, sugar, sand, fuel (rubbing alcohol).

Create a fascinating fire snake by combining baking soda and sugar.

DIY Solar Oven 2.0:

Materials: Pizza box, aluminium foil, plastic wrap.

Improve the design of a solar oven to cook food using sunlight.

DIY Glowing Water:

Materials: Tonic water, blacklight.

Discover the fluorescent properties of tonic water under UV light.

~

DIY Rainbow Fire:

Materials: Fire-resistant chemicals (e.g., boric acid), rubbing alcohol.

Create a mesmerizing display of rainbow-coloured fire.

~

DIY UV Bead Bracelet:

Materials: UV beads, string.

Make a bracelet with UV beads to detect the presence of ultraviolet light.

~

DIY Water Xylophone:

Materials: Glasses, water, mallets.

Create a water xylophone to explore sound waves and pitch.

DIY Magnetic Levitation:

Materials: Neodymium magnets, pyrolytic graphite.

Experiment with magnetic levitation using strong neodymium magnets.

DIY Water Filter:

Materials: Plastic bottle, sand, gravel, cotton balls.

Build a simple water filter to demonstrate water purification principles.

DIY Lemon Battery 2.0:

Materials: Lemons, copper and zinc electrodes.

Improve the design of a lemon battery to generate electricity.

DIY Rainbow Milk Experiment:

Materials: Milk, dish soap, food colouring.

Observe the dispersion of colours using the surface tension of milk.

DIY Smoke Rings:

Materials: Plastic bottle, balloon, rubber band, smoke source.

Create smoke rings using a homemade smoke ring launcher.

DIY Edible DNA Model:

Materials: Licorice, coloured marshmallows, toothpicks.

Construct an edible DNA model using candy and toothpicks.

DIY Fireproof Balloon:

Materials: Water, balloon, flame source.

Demonstrate the heat-absorbing properties of water by holding a balloon over a flame.

DIY Solar Water Purifier:

Materials: Clear plastic bottle, water, sunlight.

Build a solar water purifier to explore solar disinfection.

DIY Cartesian Diver 5.0:

- *Materials: Plastic pipette, water, small weights.*

- *Enhance the Cartesian diver experiment using a plastic pipette and additional weights.*

~

DIY Fire Extinguisher:

- *Materials: Vinegar, baking soda, empty plastic bottle.*

- *Create a chemical reaction to simulate a fire extinguisher effect.*

~

DIY Magnetic Train:

- *Materials: Magnets, small metal objects, track (wood or cardboard).*

- Build a magnetic train using the repelling forces of magnets.

DIY Eggshell Geodes:

- Materials: Eggshells, alum, food coloring.

- *Grow colourful crystal geodes inside eggshells.*

~

DIY Electric Playdough:

- *Materials: Flour, salt, cream of tartar, water, battery, LED.*

- *Make conductive playdough and explore basic circuits.*

~

DIY Walking Water Rainbow:

- *Materials: Water, cups, paper towels, food colouring.*

- *Observe capillary action creating a walking water rainbow.*

~

DIY Wind Energy Experiment:

- *Materials: Fan, small wind turbine model (popsicle sticks, cardboard, generator).*

- *Investigate wind energy by creating a small wind turbine model.*

DIY Solar Still 2.0:

- *Materials: Plastic wrap, container, plant material, sunlight.*

- *Enhance the solar still experiment to observe water evaporation and condensation.*

DIY Fire Tornado:

- *Materials: Metal mesh, spinning platform, fire source.*

- Create a controlled fire tornado using a spinning platform.

DIY pH Rainbow:

- Materials: Red cabbage, various household substances.

- Use the red cabbage indicator to create a pH rainbow.

DIY Cartesian Diver 6.0:

- Materials: Plastic syringe, water, small weights.

- Modify the Cartesian diver experiment using a plastic syringe.

DIY Pepper and Soap Experiment:

- Materials: Pepper, dish soap, water.

- Observe the effect of soap on water surface tension using pepper.

DIY Magnetic Field Viewer:

- Materials: Magnet, clear plastic container, iron filings.

- Create a magnetic field viewer to visualize magnetic field lines.

DIY Acoustic Levitation:

- *Materials: Ultrasonic transducer, power source, levitating object.*

- *Experiment with acoustic levitation using sound waves.*

DIY Non-Newtonian Fluid Pool:

- *Materials: Cornstarch, water, plastic pool.*

- *Fill a pool with a non-Newtonian fluid for a fun and messy experience.*

DIY Electric Lemonade:

- *Materials: Lemon, zinc and copper electrodes, LED.*

- *Make an electric lemonade battery to power an LED.*

DIY Cartesian Diver 7.0:

- Materials: Plastic pipette, water, small weights, small tube.

- Enhance the Cartesian diver experiment with additional components.

DIY Invisible Ink with Baking Soda:

- Materials: Baking soda, water, paper, heat source.

- Create invisible ink using a baking soda solution and reveal it with heat.

~

DIY Lemon Volcano:

- Materials: Lemon, baking soda, dish soap.

- Combine a lemon with baking soda to create a fizzy lemon volcano.

~

DIY Solar S'mores Oven:

- Materials: Shoebox, aluminium foil, plastic wrap, sunlight.

- Construct a solar oven to make s'mores using sunlight.

~

DIY Biodegradable Seed Starter Pots:

- Materials: Newspaper, soil, seeds.

- Create biodegradable seed starter pots using rolled newspaper.

~

DIY Thermochromic Slime:

- Materials: Thermochromic pigment, clear glue, liquid starch.

- Make slime that changes colour with temperature variations.

~

DIY Straw Oboe:

- Materials: Drinking straws, scissors.

- Create a simple musical instrument, an oboe, using straws.

DIY Ferrofluid Experiment:

- Materials: Vegetable oil, magnetite powder, magnet.

- Make ferrofluid and observe its behaviour in the presence of a magnet.

DIY Mentos and Soda Fountain:

- Materials: Mentos candies, soda, Geyser tube.

- Create a spectacular soda fountain with the Mentos and soda reaction.

DIY Rainbow Fireworks in a Jar:

- Materials: Oil, water, food colouring, Alka-Seltzer tablets.

- Create a dazzling display of "fireworks" in a jar.

DIY Magic Milk Experiment:

- Materials: Milk, dish soap, food colouring.

- Observe the mesmerizing patterns formed by the interaction of milk and soap.

DIY Magnetic Putty:

- Materials: Iron filings, clear putty, magnet.

- Mix iron filings into putty to create magnetic putty.

DIY Soap-Powered Boat:

- Materials: Soap bar, plastic container, water.

- Create a boat propelled by the reaction between soap and water.

DIY Crystal Garden:

- Materials: Epsom salt, hot water, food colouring.

- Grow colourful crystals in a garden-like formation.

DIY Glow-in-the-Dark Slime:

- Materials: Glow-in-the-dark paint, clear glue, liquid starch.

- Make slime that glows in the dark.

DIY Rainbow Milk Explosions:

- Materials: Milk, dish soap, food colouring, cotton swab.

- Create vibrant explosions of colour on the surface of the milk.

DIY Straw Rocket Launcher:

- Materials: Drinking straws, paper, tape.

- Design and launch paper rockets using a straw rocket launcher.

DIY Lemon Battery 3.0:

- Materials: Lemons, copper and zinc electrodes, LED.

- *Enhance the design of a lemon battery to power an LED.*

DIY Glowing Water Balloons:

- *Materials: Tonic water, water balloons, blacklight.*

- *Fill water balloons with tonic water for glowing effects under UV light.*

DIY Density Rainbow:

- *Materials: Various liquids, food colouring.*

- *Layer liquids of different densities to create a colourful density rainbow.*

DIY Edible Water Bottles:

- Materials: Sodium alginate, calcium lactate, water.

- Create edible water bottles using molecular gastronomy techniques.

DIY Rainbow Clouds:

- Materials: Shaving cream, water, food colouring.

- Make rainbow-coloured clouds by mixing shaving cream, water, and food colouring.

DIY Fire-Resistant Money:

- Materials: Rubbing alcohol, paper money.

- Demonstrate the fire-resistant properties of money with rubbing alcohol.

DIY Crystal Ball:

- Materials: Glass sphere, Epsom salt, water.

- Create a crystal ball by growing crystals on a glass sphere.

DIY Edible Watermelon Slime:

- Materials: Watermelon, cornstarch.

- Make edible watermelon slime using watermelon juice and cornstarch.

About The Author

Dheeraj Mehrotra, MS, MPhil, PhD (Education Management)., a white and a yellow belt in SIX SIGMA, a Certified NLP Business Diploma holder, is an Educational Innovator, Author, with expertise in Six Sigma In Education, Academic Audits, Neuro-Linguistic Programming (NLP), Total Quality Management In Education, an Experiential Educator, a CBSE Resource towards School Assessment (SQAA), CCE, JIT, Five S, and KAIZEN. He has authored over 100 books on computer science, AI, digital body language, NLP, quality circles, school management, classroom effectiveness, and safety and security. A former Principal at De Indian Public School, New Delhi, (INDIA), NPS International School, Guwahati, and Education Officer at GEMS, Gurgaon, with ample teaching experience of over Three Decades, he is a certified Trainer for Quality Circles/ TQM in Education and QCI Standards for School Accreditation/ School Audits and Management. He has also been honoured with the President of India's National Teacher Award in 2006 and the Best Science Teacher State Award (By the Ministry of Science and Technology, State of UP), Innovation in Education for his inception of Six Sigma In Education by Education Watch, New Delhi and Education World- Best Teacher Award, BOLT Learner Teacher Award by Air India, 'Innovation in Education Award 2016' by Higher Education Forum (HEF), Gujarat Chapter, among others. He has developed over 150 FREE EDUCATIONAL MOBILE Apps for the Google Play Store exclusively for Teachers, Students, and Parents. This work has been recognised by the LIMCA BOOK OF RECORDS and INDIA

BOOK OF RECORDS as the only Indian to draw that feast. As a founder and president of the IoT Society of India, he also promotes Technology Globally. Dr Mehrotra is presently engaged as a PRINCIPAL at KUNWARS GLOBAL SCHOOL, Lucknow, India. He has conducted over 2000 workshops globally on "Excellence In Education" integrated with Total Quality Management and Six Sigma, Technology Integration in Education (TIE), Developing towards being ROCKSTAR TEACHERS, including Cyberspace, Cyber Security, Classroom Management, School Leadership & Management, and Innovative teaching within classrooms via Mind Maps, NLP and Experiential Learning in Academics. He is an active TEDx speaker and can be viewed on the YouTube TEDx channel. As a premium UDEMY Instructor, he has developed over 450 courses and caters to over 8 Lakh students from 180 countries.

He can be visited at www.authordheerajmehrotra.com

Books By The Same Author

SCHOOLS
QUALITY
ASSESSMENT
AND
ACCREDITATION
(SQAA)
Dr Dheeraj Mehrotra

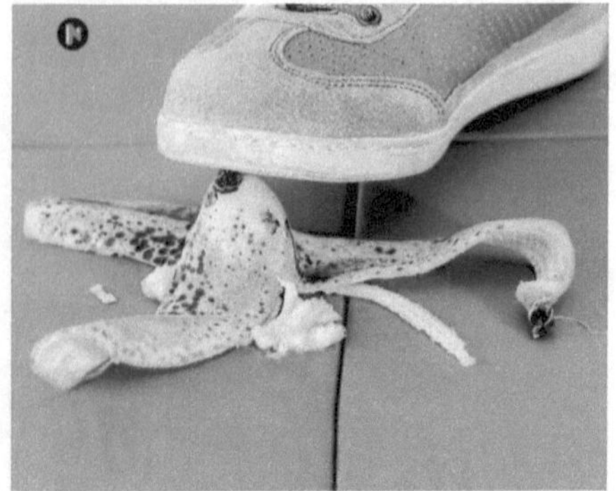

A
PRIORITY
FOR
SCHOOLS

www.authordheerajmehrotra.com

DISOBEDIENT UNDER PATRIARCHY

SAFA HUSSAIN

Made with ♥ on the Notion Press Platform
www.notionpress.com

Dedicated to my Mom. This book is Her creation.

Since She created me, everything I create belongs to Her.

Contents

PREFACE

The most egregious crime a Woman can commit under the Patriarchy is learn how to say No. I am not only teaching Women how to say No, but also making them comfortable saying No over and over again. Treat this book like a guide, a Womanifesto, or your first step into finding your personal power. Under patriarchy, Women are not allowed to defend themselves because to be honest, you cannot and should not defend yourself. Self-defense implies that you have to be attacked first. That you have to become a victim first and then let those Women empowerment quotes inspire you into smashing your attackers head on a brick wall.

Self-defense is insufficient. The only real self-defense under patriarchy is Creating Offense. You should not have to wait for a man to attack your right to life for you to tell him to go kill himself, no, constantly having to be on a self-defense mode hurts us all. You need to tell him to go kill himself regardless of if he might or might not offend a Woman. So, he hesitates attacking the Womanity ever in his life. You have to terrify him beforehand so his body shivers when a Woman is around. You have to give him the same fear that you feel as a Woman every single day. Fear cannot disappear; it can only switch sides. You do not have to wait to sacrifice a Woman, a baby, a dog, a cow, a goat, or a monitor lizard for you to yell at the top of your lungs that there is something deeply wrong with the male-kind.

But wait, aren't Women physically weaker than men? So how will that be possible?

Through this book I aim to take Women through a journey towards their own personal power that every single one of them holds within Herself.

I

Understanding the current patriarchal system

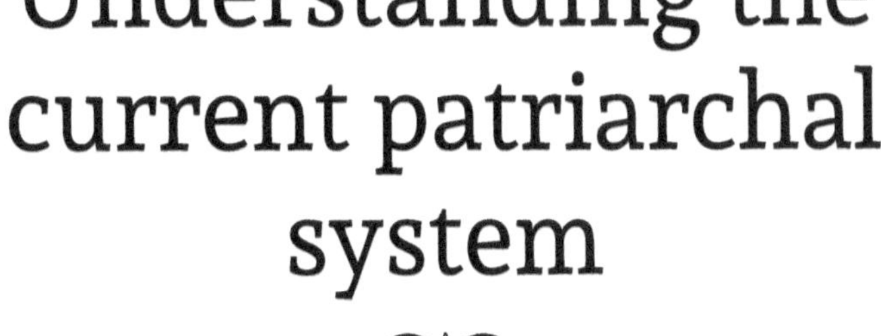

Every child is born a *tabula rasa*, a clean slate, untouched by any preconceived notions or societal influences. So, how is it that one child, years later, grows up to become a red-pilled alpha male, resolute in his belief that he is to be worshipped, while another child becomes a Woman who believes that her existence, survival, and safety depend solely on the mercy of men?

A layperson might answer, "Because of society and culture!" while someone active in Feminist spaces might argue, "It's the result of a patriarchal brainwashing." Others may contend that an unsafe society is simply inevitable. But the question remains: Who is truly to blame?

To find the answer, it's important to look at the societal framework that creates these so-called alpha bros and pick-me Women. It's about understanding how impressionable

individuals are molded into characters that seem destined to cause harm and instilling in them the belief that, because a Woman's frame has become smaller over centuries, she is inherently inferior to a male.

Before examining the system itself, we must first determine the starting point. When does the shaping and reinforcement of male superiority and male authority over everything begin? Is it when a child first gains access to social media? Is it when school teachers closely examine the length of the skirts of Female minors? Is it when they witness violence at home; seeing their Mothers beaten by their fathers, only to return to cooking dinner for them? When they see naked Women dancing on a stage surrounded by fully clothed men? Or is it when they grow up without learning that Women are a part of humanity?

The Blind leading the Blind. Our current society is ignorant. It is ignorant to the unimportance of everything they think they own and to the importance of the powers they have within themselves to create a utopia.

Let's look at the life of Vira and figure out the first moment when she was subjected to the molding process. Vira is not a Woman, or a Girl, or a toddler, or an infant. She's not even in the Womb yet! Right now, Vira is merely a plan being formed, with its outcome still unknown.

I think we should have a baby – says the strategist with a 0% contribution to project building.

What if it's another Girl? - asks the one with the entire burden of the project.

Be positive, it will be a boy – says the one who will take all the credit and ownership.

Did you notice that the first time Vira was subjected to the molding process was before she even existed? The mere thought of the to-be fetus being Vira was rejected. She

was despised even before she became Vira. She was rejected even before she had the chance to come into existence not because she was Vira, but because Vira was a *She*.

The preference for boys and men, and the disdain or avoidance of Girls and Women as coworkers, Daughters, and service providers, doesn't begin when the workday starts, or when a Woman makes a mistake, or when she disobeys as a little Girl. It doesn't even begin in childhood or in the Womb. In reality, it starts in the abstract, in the realm of thought: What if it's a Girl? What if my boss is a Woman? What if my doctor is Female?

You, as a Woman, are someone whose not only presence is rejected, but the thought of your existence is rejected too. How many of us were expected to be someone carrying balls, hanging vulnerably between our legs, while popping out of the Womb, instead of carrying Ovaries protected inside our body? I can most certainly answer 'me'.

Vira was hated and she did not even exist. She had no identity, no name, no physical body, no existence, and yet, she was already unwanted. Vira did not get the chance to make a mistake, to accidentally kill a man, to intentionally commit a double homicide, to disobey the male, or to destroy the same forces that once consumed her Mother, and yet, Vira was executed even in the realm of thoughts. Do we realize how deep the disgust and apathy towards Women is rooted in the minds of people? Does the Vira reading this realize that maybe even she was not born with the scrotum that her parents expected her to carry?

You, as a Woman, are subjected to this disdain at every single point in your life. When your teachers hold workshops telling you to dress modestly in school and not show your legs you *12-year-old whore*, you are being subjected to this disdain. When you see males saying,

"Women complain about rape yet they dance naked on reels", you are being subjected to this disdain. Men talk about rape as if it's a form of sexual attraction. Males think that rape is a form of sex, they believe that rape is a compliment, that's why to call women ugly, they call them unrapable. This is you being subjected to this disdain. The biggest trauma any woman will ever experience is being treated as a compliment by males. *Your biggest fear is treated like a fantasy by men.*

A Woman has the profound ability to create life within her body, yet she is convinced that it is her divine duty assigned by God to suppress her natural instincts, discomfort, and disgust, and offer her body whenever her husband demands it. The other, seemingly indifferent to her sensations or consent, wields his organ, the one used for both excretion and reproduction, with great entitlement. They see the world as unsafe and unstable due to men wielding power and those stripped of it. Observing this chaos, they devise what they believe is a foolproof plan to secure both their present and future. They decide to bring forth, or at least attempt to, a boy. A boy they will only nurture but not mold the nature of, the one they will let run wild with his flaws and vices, and place all their hopes of protection upon. A wayward offspring that they assume will be their own "personal monster" to help them get by in this evil patriarchal world by either fending off or aligning with other monsters. They desire a new pair of balls inside their house. They want their offspring to carry what will shrivel under cold, sag under heat, and be so utterly sensitive even the slightest flick will generate delirious and intense pain for hours, maybe days, so they can proclaim that their house is anchored by a male. The everlasting strong and powerful patriarch who not only will be their

own personal snake expected to not bite its owners, but will also be the reason why the parents will be able to say that their future is secure. My future is secure. *Now, when my son gets older, he will freely go out and make money, even his marriage alone will bring me riches. And when I die, my son will do my last rites as God intended. So much more useful than a Daughter, the one who becomes impure while her body detoxifies itself through Menstruation. My future is secure. And even after he's married, I won't be left alone. His Wife will wash my dirty dishes and change my adult diapers.*

This is life under patriarchy, male-centric brains cannot think beyond themselves.

As a Woman you're hated but you didn't terrify other people, you actually sacrificed your life and your desires to please your parents, your husband, his parents, and your children. You sacrificed your health, your mental sanity, your limited time, and your peace to conform to the idea of the self-sacrificing *Bhartiya Naari* or Indian Woman. You erase yourself to please others, but then, why are you hated?

II

Why man wants to be superior

You are hated and rejected because Femininity is a threat to the male kind, and you are the physical manifestation of Mother Nature, whether you accept it or deny it. Human males try to control nature instead of accepting its authority like the males of other species do because Nature is inherently anti-male.

Balls

Where do we begin? Mother Nature gave the male balls which hang outside his body with absolutely zero protection, made them highly sensitive, and put them at a kickable and punchable height. Balls in a male produce sperm nonstop. This nonstop production causes their body to waste energy and decay faster. This inherent defect results in males aging quickly and dying earlier. There is not a single country on earth where men have a longer lifespan than women, and worldwide statistics show that women typically live five years longer than men. The physical superiority of this sex is defeated with a simple

flick of his man-can. *This is nature.*

The male was not satisfied with this biological reality. The male, in this context, sought to dominate nature by rebranding balls as symbols of strength, power, and authority. Despite the truth that Mother Nature has presented, he has attempted to embody themes of leadership and dominance throughout all of history. *This is Patriarchy.*

"In art and culture, balls have often been associated with power and authority due to their roundness, symbolizing completeness and perfection. The use of balls in the crowns of monarchs, for example, signifies their divine right to rule and their dominion over their subjects."

Before we move forward with the absurdity of this logic, I want to know who exactly looks at something round and thinks, "This has a round shape, it must be powerful!"? Every time I look at something round, I think, "Hmm, this is shaped like a ball, it must be made for kicking."

The patriarchy rebranded balls as symbols of power and authority, and when questioned about what makes something so fragile so strong, they created numerous fabrications for their superiority. They claimed that it is round, but if roundness is the measure of strength, then wouldn't the Female body be the most powerful since Women are naturally curvier? Therefore, Black and African Women stand at the top of the hierarchy.

The truth is that the balls are not just "weak", they're highly sensitive. In fact they're so sensitive that taking a hit to the testicles does more than just knock the wind out of a male. The pain can be intense enough to double someone over, make them feel sick, or even cause vomiting. In severe cases, it may require a trip to the hospital. The discomfort isn't just localized to the groin; it often extends all the way

up to the abdomen. This is because the testicles originally develop in the abdomen before descending into the scrotum shortly before (or afterward in some premature births), bringing along nerves and tissues that cause pain to radiate through the body. The nerve fibers travel from the scrotum up the inguinal canal to their original location in the abdomen. As a result, a kick to the testicles isn't just felt locally, your brain interprets the pain as if your abdomen has been attacked.

Our bodies have built-in mechanisms to safeguard their most vital parts. For instance, the skull shields the brain, the Ovaries, essential for reproduction, are housed within the body and further protected by the pelvic bone. In contrast, testicles, which are responsible for sperm and testosterone production, are positioned externally without the same protective barriers. This makes them particularly vulnerable to injury. However, what they lack in armor, they make up for in sensitivity, packed with an abundance of pain receptors, unlike the brain.

The pain inflicted on the "please be gentle" zone isn't just a momentary discomfort or something that fades in a few hours. After the main event of a "Ball Bust" premieres, the audience sticks around for the afterparty and return gifts. The aftermath of a serious impact to the testicles can extend far beyond the initial trauma. Severe cases of ball busting can cause a man to lose consciousness as the body floods with endorphins, leading to a drop in oxygen levels. All it takes is a Woman kicking the nuts with her normal force (no special training or exhausting her body required) for a male to reach these severe levels of incapacitation. Imagine the evil angry superior patriarch, lying unconscious after you accidentally knee his nuts.

Once conscious, the "precaution package" is often left in excruciating pain, accompanied by sweating and involuntary crying in a fetal position, triggered by the activation of the cervical sympathetic ganglia.

The male might feel faint, light-headed, weak, nauseated, or even lose consciousness. This reaction, known as a vasovagal response, occurs when the vagus nerve, which helps regulate heart rate, blood pressure, and digestion, becomes overstimulated. This overstimulation can cause a sudden drop in heart rate and blood pressure, leading to dizziness or fainting. Since the vagus nerve is highly sensitive to emotional and physical stimuli, the response can be triggered by various factors such as the sight of blood, fear of injury, or in this case intense pain.

The testicles have a complex nerve structure with multiple pain pathways and a surprisingly large representation in the brain's sensory map. A light flick to the epididymis (the tube at the back of the scrotum that stores and carries sperm), could cause severe pain due to the high concentration of nerve endings in the area.

Another side effect is erratic body temperature fluctuations, which adds to the misery. The pain can last for hours, stretch into days, and in extreme cases, even linger for weeks. Random, sharp spasms and gut-wrenching aches may strike out of nowhere, serving as painful reminders of that single unfortunate incident. After all, you're attacking a major organ filled with nerve endings that travel all over the body.

If kicked hard enough, as in with your basic Woman strength, the testicles can also move back into the abdomen leaving the guy with an empty sack with his balls lodged back into the abdominal cavity. It can be relocated to the ball sack by making them painfully pass through the cavity

and into the balls, which will cause some screaming. But if the testicles stay in the abdomen, they start to die. No more sperm and testosterone. Depending on how bad the injury was, the scrotum will probably be sore for three to five days afterward. If you don't let them heal, the pain and discomfort can get worse and so can the swelling.

Getting your masculinity smashed for the first time is an experience you'll never forget and clearly not in a good way. Getting kicked in the scared sack can trigger a fountain of projectile vomit leaving you throwing up like an infant that overindulged in milk. But unlike regular nausea, this kind sticks around like an unwanted guest, leaving you dry heaving. The pain isn't just physical. It's the kind of brain-frying agony that makes it impossible to think about anything other than how much you wish you didn't carry the alleged symbol of strength. Between the sweating, the tears you didn't know you could cry, and your mental capacity hitting zero, you might just end up rolling around in your own puke, wondering if this is how it all ends.

Another consequence, far worse than the physical pain, is the crushing humiliation that comes after the male ego gets obliterated by a little Girl who mistook your balls for actual golf balls and swung a club at them. There he is, broken, defeated, and surrounded by the sound of Women laughing hysterically at the reality of how fragile the patriarchy truly is. It's not just the balls that got smashed; the male pride took a direct hit as well.

Getting hit in the testicles isn't just physically painful, it has mental and emotional effects. The immediate reaction is often a mix of shock and panic, as the sudden, intense pain triggers the body's fight-or-flight response. This can leave a male momentarily disoriented, struggling to process the overwhelming sensation. If the incident happens in

public, embarrassment can add to the distress, making the experience even more uncomfortable. "What if other Women join in as well? What if these other Girls decide to kick me too? There's nothing I can do!"

In the short term, lingering pain and discomfort can cause irritability and mood swings. Some men may become more cautious or even anxious about activities that could put them at risk of another injury. This heightened awareness can lead to an overly protective mindset, making them hyper-aware of their movements and surroundings.

If the injury is severe or traumatic, the psychological effects can be more long-lasting. Some men develop a deep fear of reinjury, leading to avoidance behaviors in sports or social situations. In extreme cases, a particularly painful experience may even contribute to heightened anxiety or mild post-traumatic stress-like symptoms, making them more hesitant about physical contact. Now imagine if I kicked a man's balls for staring at me, doing the typical Indian Male Stare, he would definitely never try to virtually rape any other Woman ever again.

A man after he experiences the agony of your shoe isn't going to develop hate for you or a feeling of revenge, but a deep fear not just from you, but from Women in general.

Haruki Murakami wrote in 1Q84, how the Female protagonist Aomame learned that, judging by the reaction of men after they get kicked in the balls, no one seems to be able to handle the pain and major loss of self-respect that comes with it. That is quite accurate, testicular pain is the most agonizing pain a man can feel physically, but it's also responsible for an extremely deep psychological pain that follows, one that is tied to the fact that your main source of pain and weakness, that reminder of your inferiority dangling precariously between your legs, is also what

makes you male. The realization that what makes you male is your weakness, your design flaw, yet for her, balls are perfectly designed.

At that moment you realize that you are not in control, you are one testicular assault away from a Woman deciding exactly what happens to you. There's a particular existential dread that comes from realizing that any Girl, regardless of strength, height, skills, or age can completely and utterly defeat you without so much as trying. That any Woman, with just two fingers, can squish one of your testicles to the point you will pass out and even risk losing that testicle forever. The thing carrying your genetic code, your reproductive capacity, your testosterone factory, all gone because a Girl wanted to, or maybe didn't, but she squeezed a bit too much by accident and now she is laughing at the squeaky sound of your manhood rupturing in her fingers. The laughter is almost as painful as the pain itself, knowing that one of the two is true: she has no idea how much pain you are in so it's just funny to her, or she knows exactly the pain she put you through and she is enjoying it. It's difficult to tell which would feel worse.

As a male, you are socialized to think that this world and everything in it was built for you. As a male, society tells you that you can be anything you want, and only YOU can be what you want, not a Woman. The world is your oyster, and you are entitled to all humanity has to offer. As a male, nobody tells you to watch over your drink, to not be alone at night, to only go out if your Sister goes with you. You don't walk around with several emergency contact strategies saved on your phone, you don't overthink if the way you are dressed can cause problems, you just exist freely in the world, taking everything for granted. It is really easy for you to let society convince you that you are superior for being born male. As a superior male, you feel

entitled to get what you want, even if what you want is other people. You are not used to suffering any consequences for your actions, and so you just act, without any fear of retaliation.

And then, for the first time in your life, it happens. A Girl kicks you in the balls. All of a sudden, all those feelings come crumbling down as her foot re-signifies your entire existence. Forget what society told you, all the lies that they told you, her foot just presented you with the real truth about your masculinity. You just came face to face of what being a male genuinely means: it means, you are not in control. It means, what makes you male makes you weak. It means at any point, any Girl, and I do mean ANY Girl, who wishes to do it, can and will leave you in a liminal state between life and death cursing the day when the Y chromosome decided you would have balls instead of Ovaries. At that moment you realize that nature made one sex to rule over the other, it made the ruling sex without design flaws like the ones that dangle between your legs. It is so humiliating that you start thinking how uncomfortable and compromising balls are for you; while also realizing how comfortable and convenient your balls were made for her. They are round, as a kickable object, they are soft and squishy, so they don't hurt her foot and can be a lot of fun along with a rush of power if she squeezes it. They are hard to defend by you, but easy to reach by her, foot, hands or knees. It's as if your balls were made for her.

"Please stop kicking my balls"

"If they're not meant for kicking then why are they shaped like a ball?" My Sister said and shoved her foot between my legs.

Balls are what make you a man. Your genetic material, your male hormones, your reproductive capability. It is also what makes you weak, controllable, at the mercy of any Woman who hasn't been cursed with the male-only weakness you carry between your legs. It feels sadly poetic that to look at them, you

must look down. Almost like you are looking down on your masculinity. You're disappointed at it.

You can be the most intelligent man you know; one hit to the balls, and your brain fries in agony, incapable of the most basic thought. You can be the strongest man you know; one hit to the balls, and your entire strength is gone and you can't even pry that small Girl's hands away from your balls. You can be the fastest man you know; one hit to the balls and your legs are shaking, powerless, unable to keep you standing up let alone run. No matter what talents or skills or power you developed as a male, the moment she hits your balls, all your accolades are gone and all you become is a whimpering mess, back to the fetal position, useless, crying, rocking back and forth, holding back nausea, trying to be able to breathe properly. At that moment you are alone with your manhood and it is screaming in pain.

The fetal position represents our most vulnerable state, the one we first experience inside a Woman's Womb. Males return to this state once they experience the agony of a Woman's shoe. It's a reminder that Women hold the power to give and take away life. In the aftermath of ball busting, it's as if Mother Nature is reinforcing this truth, that Women stand at the pinnacle of power. It's a return to the primordial truth: Women give and take life. In that moment, all social constructs and illusions crumble, leaving only the raw reality of nature, the first lesson learned in the Womb. In a way, it's a second birth. The first brought your body into the world; the second, through pain, awakens your consciousness. Your real first day, the moment you see the world as it truly is. And just like before, both births happen from the same position.

That, that moment right there, the despair and existential dread you feel when you wonder if she ruptured them, that is what being a male truly means. No matter what you do, you will never be better than what your balls are. They are

your ultimate limit, your titanium ceiling. And then, as you contemplate if death is a preferable scenario, you hear her laughter, her delightful laughter of genuine joy. She can't stop it, she can't help it, her eyes are tearing up just like yours, albeit for completely opposite reasons. Or maybe for the same reason: your balls. The moment you found out you were inferior; is the time she confirmed her superiority. Congratulations, you have finally understood the truth about what being a male means." – Testimony from a male on his perception of himself before and after experiencing the agony of a Woman's shoe.

We can clearly see the reverence this male developed for Women and the humility it developed after going through the ball busting process. Getting kicked in the balls is a curial part of a man's life.

The balls are built, naturally, to inflict as much suffering as possible to their owners. With their multiple nerve endings, the male genitalia stand undefended. Males, unlike elephants, not only have their sensitive sack hanging outside, but are also bipedal, making their groin even more vulnerable. It is also strategically positioned in a way that makes it difficult for the male to defend it, as if Mother Nature intended to ensure open access while leaving him vulnerable and unable to protect his weakness. Imagine a man trying to protect his balls from a woman. Imagine how utterly pathetic he looks as he is bowing down with a fearful expression on his face, holding his little pipe. It's as if Mother Nature designed an innate humiliation center for the male.

Come on, getting kicked in the balls won't hurt that bad – protested Vira.

Vira, one needs balls to admit that balls are anything but strong - Said Rolf.

"That time was in high school, we had just finished our English exam and we were sharing our answers and I was making fun of my friend cause her answers were so dumb, but her little Sister was so angry that I was making fun of her big Sister, that she shouted, "Stop making fun of my Sister!" and jump at me. Me, who was lying on the floor, from the bench she was standing on, and I just remember an explosion of pain as she landed both feet on my balls, then a flash of white light, then, as if I was waking up, completely unaware, I noticed my face was wet (maybe I was crying?), and I was confused and tried to get up and my legs couldn't and the pain came flashing back, and I quickly remembered what had happened. I later managed to sit down near where our group was, and she stood in front of me, her height standing was the same as mine sitting, and she told me in a mocking tone "Aw, did it hurt? Next time don't make fun of my Sister, ok?" and gave me two very soft slaps on my cheek for emphasis.

After all that happened, we still had another exam that day, a geography one, that I was usually good at, but since I had just been kicked in the balls, first, I arrived late to the class because I could barely walk, second, I couldn't focus on anything, none of the words made sense, I was still in a lot of pain. I noticed the teacher saying "five minutes left "and I hadn't answered a single question, so I just turned to the answer sheet and started to randomly pick letters for the answers of the A-B-C-D multiple choice questions. By some miracle I got a 4 out of 10 which was the minimum I needed to not fail the year, but that kick almost made me fail the entire year of school.

Sometimes I still wonder what would've happened if I actually failed that exam and had to do the whole year over, due to one little Girl's kick. And the fact that I still got scolded by the teacher for being late to the exam, but being too embarrassed to say "sorry, I got kicked in the balls and couldn't walk faster than

this, I had to stop at least three times to compose myself outside before I finally arrived back in.

One of the things that helped the Girls get away with kicking us in the balls is that no male had the courage to tell the teachers or the staff about it."

The balls are a curse for a disobedient male. The slightest flick can lead to immense pain. Why did Mother Nature put them there at such a knee-able height? So that a male is easy to control and tame.

But the male tried his level best to hide this fact, deny it, and stop Women from kicking balls. In pre-colonial India, it was very common for Women to grab a man by his balls, drag him outside, and humiliate him if he misbehaved. The British had to label these Women as savages in order to end this practice because even they didn't have the balls to fight a Woman without losing the ability to create life, or possibly lose their own as well.

Oh, the irony! More like, "because they DID have the balls".

They were so terrified of this native practice that they started to portray Indian Women as violent and dangerous in medical and legal documents. I guess the patriarchy had to set in and get into power by absolutely pushing Women out of the competition. Can balls-havers only win when Women refuse to show up for the fight?

Even after India gained independence in 1947, these colonial ideas remained in criminal law textbooks and legal commentaries and despite updates to laws about gender-based violence, these outdated ideas still influence legal decisions today, as they are regularly referenced by lawyers and judges.

In colonial law, when Women caused injury to men's testicles to protect themselves from violence, such as

domestic abuse or rape, their actions were not recognized as self-defense or resistance. This approach was very different from the requirement that Women must leave physical marks on their attacker to prove rape. However, colonial court rulings show that if there was evidence of testicular injury, Women could still face prosecution for emasculation, even though their actions were often a response to violence against them.

It raises important questions: How did men, influenced by fear of Women, become the ones to shape these laws? Why was it criminal for Women to protect themselves against sexual violence? Why were they penalized for acting on natural human instincts? And why was a Woman's instinctive right to self-defense treated as unlawful?

"But the balls hang outside because sperms require lower temperatures to exist!"

When it comes to the limited roles of the testicles in the human male body, imagine my shock when I discovered that balls prove to be ineffective at carrying out their most basic function. The testicles are tasked with storing sperm, which, in itself, is an incredibly precarious responsibility. Not only do they house the sperm, but they also house the Y chromosomes, an area where the Y faces significant risks. Exposed to the harsh conditions of the external environment, the testicles are vulnerable to constant oxidation and mutations, both of which pose grave dangers to the Y chromosome's integrity. The temperature fluctuations, the constant bombardment by free radicals, and the overall harsh conditions create an environment where the Y chromosome is susceptible to serious damage. Over time, these forces work relentlessly, causing a slow and steady erosion of the Y chromosome's functionality.

Male bodies are left largely defenseless against this ongoing genetic degradation, which only compounds the fragility of the Y chromosome. This critical vulnerability, coupled with the lack of protective mechanisms, puts the Y chromosome at an even greater risk of losing its viability.

In other words, if Mother Nature wanted, balls would be located inside the male body as well, but she didn't. The kind Matriarch wanted her Daughters to have toys to play with. As I said before, Nature is inherently anti-male.

Yes, they carry sperm. So next time be careful in a Woman's presence, she might've just read my book and wanted to try out ball busting for herself leaving you sterile for shits and giggles.

Male Fetuses struggle to stay alive in the Womb.

The male existence begins with weakness. Male embryos and fetuses are known to be weaker. In the Womb, male fetuses are more prone to undernourishment. Boys are more demanding than Girls, even before birth, which can lead to challenges. To accommodate the needs of a male fetus, the placenta (which delivers nutrients and oxygen to the baby) might have to exert more effort and enlarge as pregnancy advances. However, this increased growth of the placenta can place additional strain on the Mother's body, raising the risk of complications.

Pregnancies with male fetuses are associated with a higher likelihood of complications. Conditions like pre-eclampsia and restricted fetal growth are more common in Women carrying male fetuses than those carrying Female fetuses. Doctors suggest this may be due to male fetuses having lower resilience to stress or poor conditions during pregnancy.

Pregnancies are more likely to have bad outcomes if the baby is a boy. More baby boys than Girls are born with

growth problems and issues with their placentas. As a result, more boys than Girls die during the perinatal period (the time shortly before and after birth). Baby boys are usually born with larger head sizes but are thinner compared to Girls. This suggests that boys prioritize brain development over the growth of other organs. Since all fetuses depend on the Mother and placenta to provide nutrients, boys, who grow faster and focus on brain growth instead of expanding their placentas, take a bigger risk. This strategy makes them more vulnerable to not getting enough nutrients during pregnancy.

Wait, so men have better developed brains?! I knew Mother Nature would make up for cursing men with balls. Men have bigger brains than Women by 100 grams!

But alas, nature is Matriarchal.

It turns out that science believes 'size doesn't matter'! The 'bigger the better' was believed to be true under Phrenology. Since men have bigger brains, they're smarter than Women. Unfortunately for men, Phrenology was later labelled as a pseudo-science. The truth is that Women have 85% more brain activity than men and Women's brains are radically more active than men's. This high activity grants Women enhanced brain function in empathy, intuition, collaboration, self-control, and long-term planning, all of which make them better leaders than men.

"Women are leaders and they are wired to be leaders." - Dr. Daniel Amen

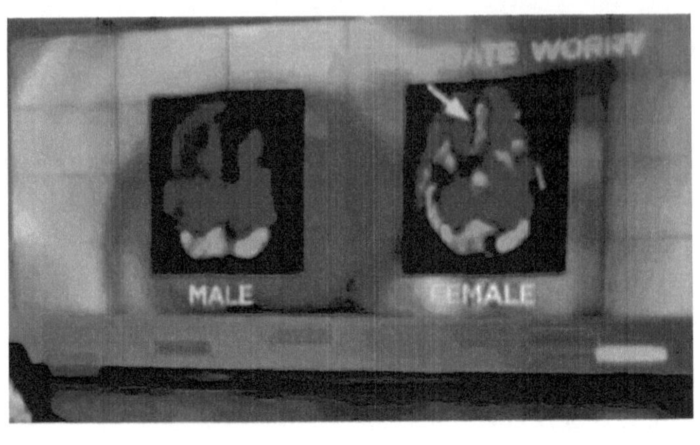

Alas, bigger isn't always better.

The male risks its life inside the Womb to ensure a good development of its brain but adult Females still have 85% more brain activity than males, risking its entire existence for nothing.

During challenging times, Women tend to naturally abort a higher percentage of male fetuses. This phenomenon is referred to as "culling" by researchers. When facing social or economic stress, a Woman's body produces more cortisol, a hormone that can be harmful to male fetuses. In response, the male fetuses may be rejected. In contrast, Female fetuses, generally more resilient, seem less affected by the elevated cortisol levels.

A new study offers support for an alternative theory: that the body deliberately eliminates male fetuses by releasing cortisol, trying to get rid of it like it was a disease, a virus, a parasite, or an infection. This could be an adaptive response, as the higher levels of cortisol might help the body reject a fetus that is less likely to survive the

challenging circumstances outside the Womb, as it is inherently weak.

Male embryos and fetuses are known to be weaker. Bringing a boy into the world during times of hardship would be less advantageous, as survival of the fittest would likely favor a Girl over a boy. Also, a Girl would be much more useful for the community, since not only is she more likely to survive, but she also has a better developed brain, a more resilient body, better communication skills, and she can produce new life as well. Whereas a male is nearly useless to the community, mostly being used for reproduction, and even then, one male could be enough to repopulate an entire village, or as expendable labor, to do dangerous work instead of Women.

The Y chromosome Loneliness Epidemic

Chromosomes are not sexes. Sexes are two reproductive strategies which produce two differently sized gametes, the male producing the smaller gamete and the Female producing the larger one. Chromosomes hold the genes which determine sex. Chromosomes are the input and sexes are the result. The SRY gene located on the Y chromosome triggers a cascade of genes leading to the Y chromosome. In its absence, WNT4 and RSPO1 lead to Female development. It's the presence or absence of the SRY gene which will determine the sex.

"What is the meaning of man?? The meaning of man is: To make a better Woman." - trustyourperceptions

The future of the male sex is becoming increasingly uncertain. One major factor is the gradual deterioration of the Y chromosome, which is responsible for determining maleness. Over time, the Y chromosome has been shrinking, losing crucial genes, and becoming weaker. Simultaneously, sperm—the vehicle that carries the Y chromosome—is also facing significant challenges. Its

motility, essential for fertilizing the egg, is declining. The combination of a deteriorating Y chromosome and reduced sperm functionality poses a serious threat to male reproduction, raising questions about the long-term viability of the male sex.

Humans possess 23 pairs of chromosomes in every cell, whether in the tongue, gut, or brain. The 23rd pair determines biological sex. In most Females, this consists of two identical X chromosomes. A person is Female if they inherit an X chromosome from both parents. This means that males, in a way, serve as a means of carrying forward the Female genetic code.

Males, on the other hand, inherit an X chromosome from their Mother and a Y chromosome from their father. The Y chromosome, which determines maleness, originates from a genetic structure with fewer resources, stored primarily in the father's sperm. Unlike all other chromosome pairs, the male sex chromosomes—XY—are distinctly different, making them the only human chromosome pair that does not mirror each other.

One significant limitation of the Y chromosome is its inability to undergo recombination with a matching chromosome. Recombination allows chromosomes to exchange genetic material, repair damage, and maintain genetic integrity. However, the Y chromosome cannot engage in this process with the X chromosome due to their structural differences. Instead of being refreshed and repaired over generations, the Y chromosome is passed down in an almost unchanged form, accumulating mutations along the way. This makes it the only chromosome in the human genome that functions in such a static and isolated manner.

Over millions of years, the Y chromosome has undergone extensive gene loss. Originally, it contained an estimated 1,000–2,000 genes, similar to the X chromosome. Today, only a small fraction of those remains functional, with estimates ranging from 27 to 45. The majority of the Y chromosome consists of repetitive sequences, with as much as 99.94% to 99.997% serving no significant function. Most of its remaining genes are focused on sperm production, further highlighting its narrowed role in biological function.

Unlike the other 22 chromosome pairs, which work together to repair damage, the Y chromosome is uniquely vulnerable. It is stored in the testes, an environment prone to oxidative stress and mutation. Because the Y chromosome cannot efficiently repair itself, mutations accumulate at a much higher rate than in other chromosomes. Each generation inherits an increasingly damaged version, making the Y chromosome one of the most degraded genetic structures in the human genome.

Due to these accumulating mutations and gene losses, some scientists predict that the Y chromosome may continue to deteriorate and eventually disappear altogether. Others argue that it has developed self-preservation mechanisms, such as gene amplification and palindromic sequences, which help slow its degeneration. However, even if it stabilizes, it will do so in a reduced and weakened state, remaining the least resilient chromosome.

Ultimately, the defining characteristic of the male sex—the Y chromosome—appears to be its greatest weakness. The very genetic structure that determines maleness is marked by loss, mutation, and degeneration. Whether the Y chromosome disappears entirely or merely stabilizes in its degraded form, it serves as a testament to

its declining role in human biology. If male extinction is a possibility dictated by nature, then perhaps it is only a matter of time before the process reaches its conclusion.

These genetic elements, which obviously show Women to be more resilient leads to one question, is misandry natural? Patriarchy is anti-nature. It's an unnatural "man-made" system, so if even Mother Nature denies it, then who are men to disagree with The Ultimate Matriarch?

Because of all these factors, men are inherently insecure. They know they're at higher risk of dying. They're closer to death and biological failure than women. A man's primary goal is ensuring his own survival.

It's fascinating how Women have been brainwashed, through religion and physical and psychological warfare, into believing that their ability to become pregnant makes them inferior and that they are physically weaker than men, or even that menstruation makes them inferior, when in fact periods protect and cleanse Women's bodies and helps them live longer. Men saw reality, created an inversion, and force-fed it to Women.

In the grand design of nature, the male faces an uphill battle for survival from the very beginning. Even as a fragile fetus, he struggles to endure the conditions of the Womb. Upon entering the world, he is conditioned to believe in his own dominance, yet paradoxically, he remains in a constant state of unease, wary of the very beings he is told to surpass. Though the unnatural order cast him as a leader, he stumbles repeatedly in a world that was never truly his to control. Meanwhile, his genetic blueprint, the Y chromosome, slowly erodes, an irreversible march toward extinction. Caught between the illusion of power and the reality of his own vulnerability, the male fights relentlessly, his ultimate goal reduced to a singular, primal instinct:

survival.

In his relentless pursuit of survival, the male gives birth to what we know today as capitalism. With survival as his primary goal, he ensures it by gaining access to as many essential resources as possible. He hoards resources. Eventually, he realizes that his hoarding has created yet another threat to his safety—other desperate males who seek to ensure their own survival. Forced to share what he once claimed as his own, he faces a new challenge. But the male humanoid, true to his nature, uses his brain which is wired for hierarchy and dominance, to seize every opportunity for profit, further expanding his *I-am-safe* survival kit.

The male puts a price tag on the resource he is forced to share, and he doesn't stop there. He convinces those beneath him in the hierarchy that *he alone* has the ability to refine and repurpose nature's raw materials because, of course, in their natural state, these resources were far too dangerous for consumption, and it is this very particular male, the one wired to be selfish, who knows how to improve a natural resource.

I mean, how could a Woman possibly know what's best for others over a man? Even if that Woman is the *Ultimate Matriarch* herself.

Remember when I said that the male tries to control nature?

The male seeks to control nature because nature itself is inherently anti-male. Likewise, he attempts to dominate Women, as they are the physical embodiments of Mother Nature. When you give Mother Nature a seed, she transforms it into a tree that bears more seeds. Similarly, when a Woman takes sperm from you, she creates a human life, which can further create life. Women are naturally

more connected to nature, inclined toward spirituality, and driven by a sense of justice in ways that men are not. All of this is determined by her prefrontal cortex. Women are wired for equality. Women are naturally resourceful, and a male being true to his nature, seeks to conquer this resource—only to repackage and sell it to her with a price tag.

Men do not hate Women because we are lesser, as we have been molded into believing, but precisely because we are better. The Crone, a book by Barbara G. Walker, talks about how in early history, 'Great Mother' religious societies, which were most societies in ancient times, males were terrified of the Female power. Men assumed that the reason Women lived longer than them was because during sex they stole men's energy. That's why men felt exhausted and lost their erection after sex, while the Women still had plenty of stamina. One of the first powers assigned to Witches was the power to steal people's energy, and it came from this feeling of inferiority that males had in the face of Women.

All this research shows is whenever a society had Women in power, males were afraid of them. Matriarchal societies were not kind societies to males, they held them by fear, and I'd assume violence to keep them in fear. "So, a matriarchal society is misandrist!!", No, they are not. Matriarchal societies do not have laws allowing grown Women to marry little boys, or allowing 50-year-old Women to have any sort of sexual relations with little boys. In fact, they don't even have any Women wanting to sleep with a minor. Keeping the gender that produces the most baby touchers in check only seems like discrimination to the one who want to touch kids.

The idea that Women would feel less exhausted than men makes sense naturally given that balls are a high energy consuming and wasteful factory. The male body is designed to spend all available energy into that one ejaculation as if it was his last. Meanwhile, the Female body already has all its eggs, it doesn't "produce" anything during sex, because everything is already there before the sex even begins. Women just enjoy sex, while sex for males is a labor they must succeed in accomplishing. The male body also releases hormones to calm him down afterward. The exhaustion from the loss of energy, combined with these calming hormones, explains the pathetic sight of a man who falls asleep right after sex. Or how men can't have sex twice in a row before taking a break. The Female body, unlike the male body, is designed for sexual pleasure. Women possess multiple organs dedicated to experiencing pleasure, most notably, the clitoris, whose sole purpose is to provide sexual enjoyment. Now, consider the male body: he experiences sex through the same organ he urinates from, and his orgasms inevitably produce sperm, regardless of whether reproduction is the goal or not. It's as if Mother Nature is sending a message—that his body isn't made for pleasure but for reproduction, with orgasm serving merely as a catalyst for fulfilling that biological duty. Men can ejaculate after a particularly brutal crushing blow to the nuts too, it is men's survival mechanism, that it's afraid that he will lose his balls and the ability to reproduce, so it desperately tries to give it a last shot at reproduction before it loses its ability to do so. In this light, it seems men are the true 'baby machines' they often claim Women are.

The hatred Women get from men is not because males think Women are so inferior to them or that they are disgusted by these lesser beings. No, he hates her out of jealousy because he deeply understands he is inferior to her

in every way. He resents her superiority, because he knows there is nothing he can do to be on her level. He has been cursed with balls for life, condemned to an insignificant and expendable existence. Imagine the feeling of learning a Girl can grab and squeeze one of your balls for as little as six seconds and you are guaranteed to lose consciousness from the intense pain? The existential crisis acknowledges that inferiority. I'm truly amazed that the sex that had to deal with the existential crisis that a little Girl can make him agonize until unconsciousness or possible death just by crushing one ball with her fingers, manages to pack up so much denial as to create the myth that they were superior and strong. However, once you remind them of that, they can't deny it anymore. So, males try to bring Women to their level, since they can't ever rise to her level.

III

The Beta Male Complex

A man is exactly like balls.

I don't know how to put it lightly and say it in a way that doesn't offend a man, but a man is, in fact exactly like balls. They're weak, fragile, bad at doing the one job they have, and highly sensitive. A man in his true nature is this. He is balls. And maybe the reason I can't find a way to say this without offending men is the same reason we haven't figured out how to flick balls without it hurting, because, no matter how gently you do it, pain is inevitable.

Men are in a constant dick swinging competition with each other. They are constantly measuring each other's dick size and comparing them to their own. A man having a bigger house in a nicer area adds 2 inches to his pecker. Men have created hierarchies among themselves on the basis of their dick sizes. How many of us are aware of the constant alpha versus beta battle going around, especially online? Us as Women find it stupid because we are not being operated

by a constant alarm system telling us that time is running out and that we are dying, we genuinely experience calm and bliss. Men don't.

Alphas, betas, sigmas, these are nothing more than labels labelled to men by men, and interestingly enough, every man is an alpha according to himself, and every other male who isn't him is a beta. They don't even have the Ovaries to admit and accept where they fall on the hierarchical pyramid, so he acts from a place of denial towards his inferiority. Though on the inside, every man realizes how much power and authority he truly holds.

What does this male made hierarchy look like? Before we move forward, I want you, Woman, to determine what would make someone the 'best' and another the 'worst', according to you? Not in the context of what you have learnt about men so far but according to you, who should be treated as an 'authority' and who should be a learner and a follower.

When we look at the Girlstagram, we see Women constantly leveling the uneven ground of inequality which includes addressing Women's issues, the issues of the Gay Community, and issues of other oppressed minorities in the most unique and creative way possible, spreading good and positive vibes while also getting their message across. Sometimes including men's issues too, which I find slowly diminishing among Women because they're finding out that men are never satisfied.

The Girls on Girlstagram keep it real with each other. They say, "Hey look, don't compare yourself to me or other Instagram models. I've had tons of plastic surgery to look this way. By the way, this is me without makeup or filters. And oh, these aren't my natural hair." They embrace every kind of Girl, Girls who love makeup, Girls who love

skincare, Girls who love making money, Girls who love reading, and Girls who love Girls. They hype up even the silliest hobbies and strive to create a judgment-free space.

The Girls on Girlstagram are also always on the lookout for other Women. They encourage each other to set aside personal differences and be there for one another, especially in times of crisis, most often, that crisis being an untamed male. It's all about having each other's backs, creating solidarity in the face of struggles that challenge their collective empowerment.

The only time a Girl might face temporary rejection is when she's being a pick-me. Any act of disobedience to the Girls' Girl movement is discouraged and called out. The Girls aim for equality because Women are wired to build social harmony.

Oppressing others, bullying, or tearing down Women of other races, religions, class, or on the basis of other factors is met with criticism. There is no hierarchy of superiority or inferiority among Women, those are patriarchal constructs that breed inequality. But the most loved Women? They're the ones who spread the most love and smiles.

Scrolling through the Girlstagram is truly soothing.

Note that what I describe next is nothing more than the description of how the Manosphere thinks and works. I do not support racism or racial superiority of any kind. The following information is based on stereotypes that the Manosphere follows and how it affects their behavior. The stereotypes may or may not have anything to do with reality. Also, note how I only needed to add a disclaimer before describing the manosphere and not the Girlstagram.

The Manosphere, on the other hand is built different, or rather is built true to its nature.

Why are some men more barbaric than others? Why are men savages at all?

Every man aims towards becoming more and more powerful and authoritarian, Women cannot understand this constant struggle and desire to be seen as the most powerful in the room. Every man, no matter what stage of success he is at, only wants more power and control. They collect accolades, they group up with other men they're similar to, and combine their accolades to maximize the size of their penis. White men take credit for what other White men have achieved in the past, Black and Pakistani men take credit for generally being perceived as attractive to Women and having high testosterone levels, Muslim men are united with their Ummah, at least united against their non-believing enemies, and have control over multiple countries. Every race or community of men has accolades which they share among each other in order to further elongate the size of their penis and take up more space in the Dick Swinging competition which is responsible for creating the said pyramid of hierarchy.

Men fixate on authority precisely because they lack it. They were never meant to lead. Void of character and skill, yet they cling to power with white-knuckled desperation, terrified of its loss. Their obsession with control is nothing more than a mask for their weakness, a futile attempt to gather enough power to erase their own fragility. What have men done with power, after all? Introduce bills to lower the age of consent to nine. But no matter how much they grasp, they remain weak. Men, like balls, are forever fragile and incapable of true strength. The whole reason why this competition exists in the first place is because of the male's constant feeling of insecurity.

The winner of this competition is usually the one who has oppressed the most, the one who stole the most, and

conquered the most. He might have killed the most, bought and sold the most, and as comes with the penis package, raped the most.

(Note, that on an individual level, a man from a lower level might outmaneuver one from a higher level, but such cases are extremely rare, almost as if I'm giving them a benefit of the doubt. The hierarchy will be described from a general perspective in the following paragraphs.)

Let's look at the various levels of the hierarchy. We won't be going through every single level of it, but only through the main three in order to understand how the hierarchy works.

The White

The dick swinging hierarchy is like a mountain, white on top. White men are considered the most powerful men because they are considered attractive, white countries are usually rich, and have a "powerful" past where they successfully colonized half the world and owned other men. Now, in the Woman's world being a colonizer is shame worthy, but in the man's, being a conqueror is being powerful. White men have their self-esteem secure due to the actions of their forefathers. They did secure resources for themselves. After the imposition of White and European features as the beauty standard, everyone else collectively see the white skin as the epitome of beauty, unless we are trying to unlearn this racist belief.

We all are aware of the term White Supremacy, the White being the "right". The White is the most superior one in the pyramid of hierarchy in the manosphere because they have almost everything necessary to survive. In the past, White men successfully colonized half the world leading them to loot and further hoard resources. They're considered the most attractive. Most White men come from

first world countries with a good global impact. Religion might play an important role in further building their self-esteem as well. The real accolade here isn't the money or the impact, it is the fact that they're what they think a Woman would want. They feel secure because they feel they're the most attractive to Women and have the most access to Women. White men stand on the top of this Pyramid.

So, the actual accolade here is the increase in the chances of getting access to Women after securing resources. The male knows that he is inherently useless and expendable. His job of providing sperm for creating life is replaceable and can be easily done by other men. One man can repopulate an entire village, so he feels insecure because he knows his life has little to no meaning unless he tries to provide a meaning for it. He aims to provide meaning to his life by stacking accolades on top of his pecker and making it longer so that more Female humans love and accept him, or as his brain tells him will happen. *Talk about being a pick-me.*

The Brown

When it comes to Brown Men, there are various factors that strongly divide them further. The first and most important factor being religion. Brown men are not similar to white men at all. Their skin looks different, their culture looks different, and their religion is also mostly different. Brown men are unable to steal self-esteem from White Men as they see White Men as a competition due to a lack of similar factors. The only time a Brown Man might take credit for a White Man's achievement is when he is battling against Women over gender.

The Brown: Muslim

Religion serves as a powerful unifying force within this community. Despite internal differences, when faced with

the non-believing Kufaar, solidarity prevails among Muslims. For the Muslim man, self-worth is often tied to the legacy of conquest. Much like the white man, they, too, have invaded nations, plundered resources, and spread their beliefs by force. In the manosphere, dominance and power over others are celebrated, and the brutal enforcement of religious control only amplifies this sense of superiority. The fact that, to this day, Muslim men will resort to violence, beheading those who challenge their faith, elevates their perceived power, inflating their fragile egos. The rule of the Taliban and other male-dominated regimes is not seen as oppression but as a triumph. The control of Women is a source of pride, and men across ideological and religious lines have expressed admiration for the Taliban's rollback of Women's rights. This male-driven worldview revels in oppression, in a society where grown men barter away their 6-year-old Daughters for wealth and survival. A country where Women are forced into anonymity under layers of fabric is met not with concern, but with applause. The more a man can control, the stronger he is considered, even if said control is bearing bitter fruits. The suffering this creates is irrelevant to them, because, in the male psyche, the only thing that matters is their own power and control. The Taliban brought to the male a sense of pride, that I, a man, control Women in Afghanistan.

When a group of untamed men go out and wreak havoc against Women, it benefits all men.

The history of the male is the history of trying to tame nature. Since Women are the expression of Mother Nature, the male seeks to tame it as well. He sees both nature and Women as forces far beyond himself. He will never feel fully secure if these forces are left to rule him over. His denial of their supremacy over him makes him forever miserable in his quest for a power

he will never possess.

Men take pride in having power and being in a position to exploit their power because to a male, the most important thing ever is ensuring its own survival. Being in power means being secure.

The Muslim Man also gets his self-esteem from his religion telling him that he is the one following the correct religion and the non-believing Kufaar will burn in hell, meanwhile he will enjoy all that his religion told him to avoid on earth, in heaven. When an Indian Muslim man feels ashamed of his identity as an Indian, he may identify more with the Ummah. For Muslim men, or any men, invading a country and committing genocide can be seen as a moment of pride for them. They are not ashamed, as a Woman would assume they'd be, but they're proud of being conquerors. Terrorist organizations, the ones that behead the non-believers, brings a sense of power and superiority to the males of this community, however this particular excuse for feeling powerful also brings shame to them in front of the men above him because they still cannot fight his alphas, the ones above him usually have the ability to end them, and use political correctness as a tool to further break him. He flexes this violent dominance only in front of the men below him.

The ultimate goal of the dick swinging competition is to defeat other men. What else would make a male seem more powerful than literally defeating another male through physical violence? Having a collective of men who wreak havoc on your behalf is nothing less than a reason of celebration for men.

If men want to defeat other men, why don't they hit each other in the balls during a fight? - asked Ana

Because fights are supposed to make them look almighty and powerful, and not pathetic and weak, like they would look in ball agony - Replied Vira

The Mus/Arab male also gains alpha points for not taking dowry but instead paying Mehr to the bride and also paying for the entire wedding. In the Indian subcontinent, the Woman is supposed to pay the man dowry to marry him and also pay for the entire wedding. Notice how there have never been any Mehr deaths but we still see dowry deaths till today.

MusRab Men are also considered attractive, and usually have big Penises, making them more desirable to Women. The Muslim/Arab Brown, also secured a good position in the dick swinging competition.

SIZE MATTERS:
Measuring Dicks Around the World

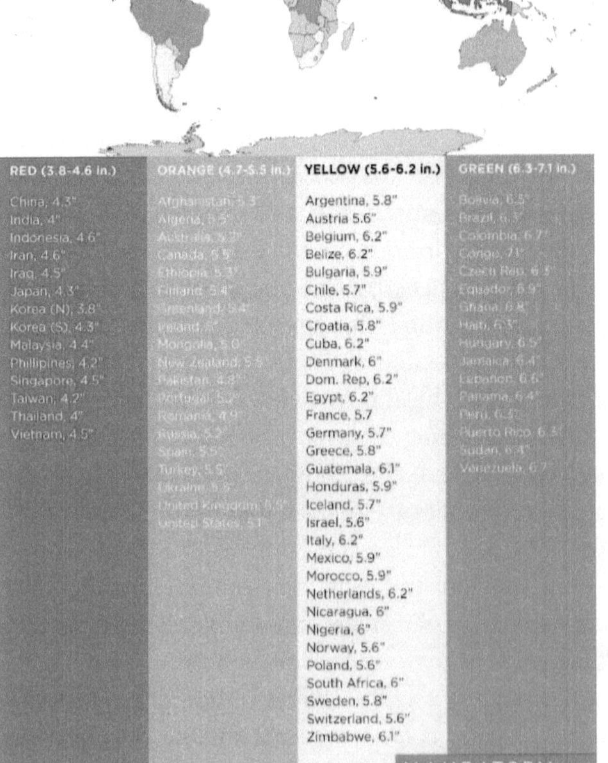

However, it is important to keep in mind that the description of the various dickerarchal strata is based on the stereotypes that the manosphere follows which may or may not have anything to do with the reality.

The Black

Black men have been conquered by both the White and the Arab. Both the White and the Arab man bought and sold the Black man as slaves. One would expect that the Black man loses the dick swinging contest due to this, but they do not. With their big penis sizes, superior physical strength, and high testosterone levels, Black men still secure a position in the dick swinging contest. When we talk about the manliest man ever, we think of a tall, dark, and a handsome man. Black men are also the trend setters and have the ability to influence cultures. Black nationalism teaches Black men that they are the cradle of civilization, that the first civilizations in the world emerged from Africa (Egypt for instance), that he has a proud history, that he was king, so he finds his self-esteem in history, bringing him inner power and strength. Although, the Black man was conquered, he still manages to keep his manliness to himself. After being conquered by the White and the Arab, they don't become the complete loser at the end as one would expect, because there are multiple sources of pride there. Black men secure an okay position in the Dickerarchy but still lean downward. However, they do show symptoms of a defeated male. Being racist against the Women of your own race is one of those.

Every man is a savage, unless trained to be otherwise, his natural tendency is savagery. He is drawn to having radically more animalistic instincts than a Woman. This barbarianism stems from his constant feeling of insecurity. He is uncertain of his own survival. His behavior is that of an animal who does

not know where the next meal is coming from. He guards the few dregs of what he has as if another man is on his way to steal it. He is insecure about what he has, because what he has is never enough. He constantly wants more. He keeps stacking his pecker up until the men around him are starving to death, but he is still not satisfied. He could still use some more.

How does it affect Women and why should Women care about men's accolades?

The real deal here isn't to understand how the "alphas" of the dickerarchy act or behave. They possess the least level of threat to Womanity, but threat is still there. Power, authority, and control over resources does make a man much more secure, but a man with his entire self-esteem to himself is still not an angel. A man who stands on top of the Dickerarchy is a lesser barbarian than those below him. He is still insecure but not completely. After all, he is still a male, so if he can't compensate for social insecurity, there is nothing he can do about his ontological insecurity.

Every man believes that he is born to rule the world. Him having access to power and resources is obvious to him. That of course I'd have access to everything I can put my finger on. When he goes out and wins, it's obvious to him. Getting what he wants makes perfect sense to him, which is why it is so important to defeat a male and crush his ego, because his ego and entitlement is the foundation of his harmful behavior. A man with his self-esteem intact is a barbarian of the lowest strata. He feels secure to a large extent in comparison to the males who are below him.

Then we move forward and look down and see men sitting in a dark corner devoid of what their minds promise them of. He also believes that he is born to rule the world, but the world is spitting in his face. The world has rejected and humiliated him because a better set of men exist out

there somewhere. The same set of men, who's accolades he flexes when involved in a gender conflict with a Woman, became the reason for his own extinction. The alarms of danger set off in his brain. His insecurity fully reveals itself, naked and unprotected, because it has nothing to hide behind. He is devastated and in shock, resulting in rage filling the void. A fire ignites in his chest, not born of courage, but from fear. He lashes out, not because he is powerful, but because he is powerless.

This man possesses absolutely no qualities to put him above another male in the Dickerarchy or to make him more appealing to Women. This male, or the community of these men, on an average would be short, because being bigger adds alpha points, not close to the European beauty standard in anyway, considered ugly, come from a dirty poor country or background, his national or religious community has never conquered any other community, his penis size falls among the bottom four in the world, and is internationally humiliated by other men who are also looking to secure their own spot in the upper strata of the Dickerarchy. A man, who is already so insecure about himself, feeling even more unsafe due to securing the last spot in the Dickerarchy, how savage will he be? What level of barbarism will this rejected creature possess? What will be his traits? Will he be destroyed?

The Dickerarchy was created in the past 2,000 years when men were in complete power, so, everything each country or community managed to gain or lose is seen as men's fault. Men will often blame Women for their downfall, but this is another attempt to ensure their own survival against Women. Men know about this Dickerarchy and how men are completely responsible for it.

This is the type of man who will display nothing but insanity while being diagnosed as mentally fit. One might stand clueless as to what exactly he is talking about all the time. Men like this tend to be deluded. Worried about a Woman using him for the money that he does not have, wanting a housewife when he does not own a house, taking pride in the civilization he built while the rest of the world sees the said civilization as a failure, taking pride in his superiority in front of fellow men of his strata because no other man would ever acknowledge what isn't there. He has no power. He has never asserted any dominance, the same dominance that all men seek. In fact, he had the men of the higher strata of the Dickerarchy assert their dominance onto him over and over again, approximately 50% of the Dickerarchy-creating time. He has no accolades to his name. He knows that he is a loser, but since his animalistic instincts are so strong, he never accepts his inferior position in the pyramid so instead, he forms layers of ego to protect himself. So, just like every male denies his inferiority to every Woman, the beta male denies his inferiority within the males. *Ego only collects at places where love is absent.* He has never really experienced power because of which he actually suffers from an inferiority complex. He is the beta male of the manosphere. He is the beta male of the Dickerarchy. He is rejected by Women. He is also rejected by other men.

This man's rejection of his inferiority is the root cause of his behavior. This man is sexually destroyed. His sexual destruction begins with constant rejection by Women. Since Women are not attracted to men they feel unsafe around, they reject him. Even if one or two do get manipulated into being with him, the relationship is short lived and is toxic in its entirety. This man is not only

rejected by Women but by society too. Society criticizes defects like him. The society imprisons mistakes like him. He believes that he too is born to rule the world but the constant rejection of his strongest belief perplexes him. He believes that the world has gone astray. Where they should spend their time worshipping him, the world is focused on itself. What do you mean Vira can choose what to wear? Today she will choose what to wear, tomorrow she will choose who to sleep with. And if Vira gets to choose who to sleep with, she would never accept me in her sheets. No, this is insanity. This must stop. No wonder males invented arranged marriages, because it's the only way they could get a wife, by force. He would never be chosen by Women naturally. He wants to 'fix' the world and take it back to a time where he could grope any Woman he wants. He wants to be applauded for making as many Women uncomfortable as possible. He wants to be rewarded for punishing Women for leaving their homes. But the world told him, no. He was again rejected.

This man finds himself lonely. So alone that even the lines of his palm are fading away, he has no future. So, he pairs up with other lonely men from his strata. Usually, a man like this also finds comfort in ideologies that validate his loser experiences. *A Woman's first God on Earth is her husband. It says right here in this Holy Book, you whore.* These victims of the Male Loneliness Epidemic come together to stroke each other's egos, like bro-therapy, holding each other's peckers and letting it know that *'hey little guy, I might not be the one you wanted but I am here for you. I know you're lonely and so am I, but it's their fault for rejecting our fondue of smegma'.* He hates Women. He hates Women not because they reject him, but because he is unable to hate on anyone else. If he went to battle a White man, he'd lose

even before trying, the Muslim would bring up the past, and the Black will flex his muscles. This man wants to release his aggression that was reserved to defeat other men. But since he already stands defeated because of his identity, like a true beta male, he launches his anger towards Women. Perhaps because he blames Women's rejection for his low position in the male rivalry. Ultimately, men prove they are better than other men by showing how many Women they have access to, because they feel superior by having access to the superior beings. Since the beta has no access to Women, he feels inferior, and thus rages against Women who he blames for that fact. This is the Beta male Complex.

The Beta not only rages against Women because he blames her for his downfall, he is angry at other men as well. He would rage against a dog too, but he chooses Women. He chooses Women not because their frame became smaller over centuries, but because right now, Women are taught fear. Women are taught not to fight, but only run away. At most, Women are being taught self-defense and never offence. Women are not naturally defenseless, but are molded in a patriarchy to be defenseless. The Beta attacks Women because there is the least resistance.

This male suffering from a Beta Male Complex hates on Women because he has no other option. He wants to feel powerful, so he attacks the ones who are not even a part of the Dick Swinging competition. He hates on what he had to convince himself was actually lower than him because that's all he can do. He spent his entire life seeking the validation of Women, being jealous of their power and superiority, and yet upon rejection had to tell himself that these Women are actually below me. *The grapes are sour.* This man is very alone, very weak, very deluded, very

sensitive, very fragile, very easily triggered, very rejected, and very invisible, and yet he is true to his nature. He is invisible to the point where one might even find his insignificant penis erect inside of a monitor lizard.

This Beta Male Complex drives them into hating themselves further and feeling even weaker in front of other men. What could be worse? Their mind is constantly telling them that they're in danger. They are insignificant and they know it. They are rejected and they know it. And to numb the pain of being the least likely to survive the agony of the natural order they convince themselves that there's another candidate for death, the Women of his own kind.

Men of all strata are violent against Women, but this Beta's violence is different. This Beta is racist against the Women of his own race. He will be seen in his corner of misery spewing racism against the Women of his own race. Often rebranding what his alphas say to him.

These men have absolutely lost the dick swinging competition. He stands no chance in a battle with any man. If he goes out to battle a male of the higher strata, he will immediately be met with slurs and insults thrown at his face. Being this man is the ultimate insult and usually the only insult they have for others is "you and I are not much different" even being compared or similar to them is an insult. "You and I are not much different" is also their subconscious belief of inferiority slipping out. The same belief that they will never admit out loud due to a lack of Ovaries to do so.

But this beta still wants to feel powerful. *Why? He has absolutely lost to other men, why can't he just accept his defeat and sit in a corner waiting for his miserable life to end?* In order to accept a situation and a condition as it is, one requires the ability to look within. In order to look within,

one requires self-awareness. A self-aware person is someone who is aware of her actions. She is not controlled by her instincts and her actions are not mere responses to triggers. A self-aware person understands that her actions have consequences and she can also differ between good and bad consequences.

Someone with no self-awareness lacks the ability to look within. Men lack the ability to look within and hence they deflect. No matter what the argument is about, their immediate reaction is to deflect whatever was said.

I did not like how you insulted me in front of your friends.
Well, what about what you did?
You raped a Woman who was going back home from work.
She was wearing a short skirt clearly asking for it.
According to him, his hands are always clean.

A man is not self-aware, because not being self-aware to him is a defense mechanism. He, in his true nature, is barbaric. He knows subconsciously that the havoc he wrecks, or desires to wreck, is evil and wrong. He hates himself. If he ever looked within or came face to face with his inner demons, he would explode. Exploding or ceasing to exist is a man's biggest and only fear on earth as his biggest and only goal is to stay alive and ensure his own survival.

This is why every time, you as a Woman, criticize men in any way, instead of empathy, you are met with a man practicing self-defense. As a victim of any form of oppression, it is normal for the oppressed class to hate their oppressors. The oppressed class is allowed violence and can never oppress its oppressors. But guess which oppressed class is denied even the right to mourn for the oppression of its class? Women. You make one simple statement 'men need to stop raping Women' and you are labelled a "misandrist" who generalizes men and hence is

as evil as the man who raped a 6-month-old baby. But the fact of the matter is, that you, as a Woman, can hate men and even act violently towards them unprovoked and you still are not an oppressor, because in a patriarchy, you are oppressed.

And thus, he fulfils his long-lost desire of feeling powerful by being an aggressive animal and a hater to the Women of his own kind like a true Beta Male.

But does unleashing aggression onto Women somehow compensate for his rejected manhood? Absolutely not. While controlling Women might earn him approval within the manosphere, because gaining control over a much superior force is alpha points worthy, much like the Taliban's oppressive rule, this rejected beta can't even manage that. Spewing disgust toward Women isn't control, it's just repulsion. Their resentment and hostility don't inspire fear or submission; instead, they look like a child throwing a tantrum because his diaper is full. *Who would be mad at an infant who is smothered in his own shit?* Women don't see them as dominant figures but as pathetic, embittered individuals grasping at a false sense of authority. In the end, their attempts at control are nothing more than public displays of failure, loud, bitter, and ultimately ineffective. In reality, he accomplishes nothing except making Women despise him even more, as he's often found getting beaten up, either by a group of men or by a single Woman.

The manosphere's obsession with controlling Women stems from a deep-rooted fear, because Women are inherently more powerful and superior to men.

Do you know any men suffering from a Beta Male Complex?

IV
Testicular Terrorism

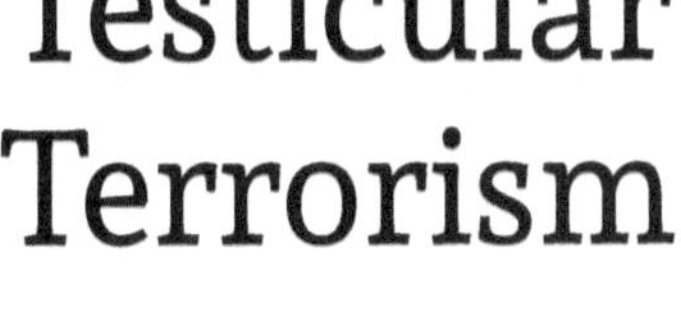

So, if men are inherently evil, shouldn't we just leave them as they are? Shouldn't we just accept the male human for who he is and set high standards for Women instead to be perfect since she is biologically superior with her 900 genes in the X chromosome and 85% higher brain activity than a man? Sounds exactly how the current society is moving.

A dog is also naturally wired to shit anywhere it likes, do we let it shit inside the house or do we train it?

One might assume after gaining this information about men, that men are just being true to their nature. They're just true to how Mother Nature wired them to be. So, why criticize something for being in its natural state? Being wild seems to be a man's natural state and he seems unable to make better decisions, so wouldn't it be unwise to hate a wild horse for running free in the jungle as nature intended?

Absolutely! After you get to learn about the male nature, the male brain wiring, and how the male's biggest challenge and goal in life is to ensure his own survival, it becomes hard to hate them. Hate stems from fear and once you get to learn about your own superiority over a man, it becomes hard to feel afraid of them.

Learning about the Female superiority and the male inferiority, under patriarchy, is like seeing the light at the end of a long torturous tunnel along with dispelling of the darkness. It is very freeing to be a Woman learning about the reality of Women and males, because the truth is on your side.

You don't have to lie, you don't have to make things up, you don't have to pretend to be what you are not, you just have to exist as a Woman and that's all. Imagine the male curse of having to pretend and falsify reality all the time so that nobody realises how weak and inferior you actually are. That life in itself must be hell, you are living afraid of reality and having to fight against nature at all times just to maintain your tiny grasp at the illusion of power, just to keep the illusion that you are not expendable with the most insignificant need.

In order to fix the current system, which you clearly are capable of, you need to first let go of your own mental shackles. You cannot create a positive change while functioning in fear. A mind functioning in fear cannot be trusted to make sane decisions. You as a Woman, suffer from a fear of males. You are afraid of being rejected by males. Afraid, not because it might have a direct impact on your self-esteem, but because his rejection might lead to you ending up in a hospital counting your last breaths. A man's rejection of his wife, because he's sick of being a husband and a father, might lead to another case of femicide, the wife turning into just another stat for the world to maybe not even care about. This patriarchal

system has led Women to feel nothing but fear of the male. First, she's told to idolize the male and follow his lead blindly as she's incapable of thinking as efficiently and smartly as a man can, just to realize that the one she's supposed to be a follower of has crossed all levels of insanity. When Women are told that men are their protectors and providers, that Women can and are supposed to depend on a man, just to end up realizing that she also needs to teach her 10-year-old Daughters about good and bad touch because there's same men around, it does create a state of mental anguish. Being told that the one who is the most likely to end up a pedophile is above her, takes a direct hit on her self-esteem. Before she feels afraid of men, she loses her confidence. How come is there a radical difference between her observations of the reality and the reality that she's being told exists?

She's afraid of men, and men are in absolute power being worshipped by everyone even after causing trauma to every living being on planet, including nature. She's functioning in fear and confusion, but lucky for her, she's found a movement which claims to set her free from this oppression. So, she joins this movement and becomes a feminist. She becomes a feminist who herself doesn't believe in her own power. She steps out to empower other Women while being anything but powerful herself. A Woman like this might have the best intentions at heart, but she cannot bring any positive change. Her mind is afraid and she will teach other Women fear.

She notices the backlash that this Female-only movement is receiving from the male. In fact, a bunch of Women also stand besides those men. Her self-esteem is again affected. Growing up brainwashed to be nothing more than a servant to a man, even she felt a sense of

unease while being treated as a priority somewhere. After all, this bitch was created to guard her master, how dare she deviate from her life's only aim?

She's not just uneasy, she's afraid of the man. And because of that fear, she devises a solution, blending her uneasiness and caution to protect herself and her Sisters. But she does so carefully, ensuring she doesn't provoke him, because in her eyes, an angered man is the source of all problems. His ego must be protected at all costs if she wants to survive. She is unaware that a man is not like a Woman, and with the ignorance of the differences between the two, she treats a man like she would treat a Woman.

She includes men into her activism and pretends to care about his issues. Since she's brainwashed into thinking that prioritizing herself makes her a wicked Woman, she convinces herself that feminism is for "everyone", hence not caring about the very person who's the reason for the creation of feminism in the first place would make her a bad feminist. She yells out "feminism is for men too!" with a huge smile on her face and pride on her chest as she's now found the cheat code to ending male violence against Women and protecting her ego which is telling her that she failed as a Woman.

She falls back into her conditioning of pandering to the male. She is stern in her belief that since she would be grateful if someone cared about her issues, the man would also see her pandering as an act of good will. Little did she know, the man sees her pandering as something obvious, in fact it's the inclusion of Women in feminism that doesn't make sense to him at all. The entire world is created to be subordinate to a Him not a Her.

Imagine someone is beating you for hundreds of years. You're hurt and broken, your self-esteem is shattered, and

you feel like you're a nobody as an individual. Now if you turn around and tell the person who's beating you, "this isn't you. You're acting this way because of something else. You're not inherently evil. I still care about your issues." How would he feel? How would the person with his shoe on your neck feel? How would it make you look?

When you turn around and tell your oppressor that you care for him and will fight for his issues, to put it in simple terms, you look like a loser. You look and act like the typical loyal bitch that men claim Women are. Are Women rightfully called bitches? Are we the most loyal pets that men have?

No, you cannot fix him with your love and kindness, the same way you can't fix a wild dog with love and kindness. You have to tame it. You have to show it the fear of consequences.

You cannot prove to a man that you're a good bitch so don't whip me. That you're not trying to overpower him, and that you're okay with the chain around your neck, but just be kind with your orders. Although the desire to be treated well is praise-worthy, you found self-respect in a system designed to destroy you, it's still not enough.

When you turn around and pretend to care about his issues, he is not experiencing gratitude, but you're adding to his entitlement. You're giving him reasons to like you, maybe because you somewhere believe that the reason why men don't like Women in the first place is Women's fault, but what you're doing is giving him reasons to become even more vile. He thinks I can rape, murder, and enslave Women and their children for centuries, and they would still care for me, that's awesome! Unknowingly you're adding to the very toxic patriarchy that you're trying to dismantle. All because you were functioning in fear.

A Woman's biggest enemy is her own fear which leads her to overestimate the male. You cannot end male violence against Women without being a violent destructive force yourself. Step one of bringing outer change is to embody the said change within yourself first. Women need to let go of their own patriarchal brainwashing while also realizing that it's a continuous process and not just a conscious decision made once in order to dismantle the patriarchy in the outer world. Once you realise your true potential as a Woman, an angry hateful misogynistic man starts to look like a toddler crying because his diaper is full. He seems funny, miserable, pity worthy, and his behaviour also seems predictable. So why would the mature adult be angry and fazed by a toddler throwing a tantrum because he's smothered in his own shit?

Until you do not reach the state of seeing misogynistic men as toddlers, you're not in touch with your personal power and cannot empower Women further.

Mary Anne Franks in men, Women, and Optimal Violence talks about how in order to end male violence, we should not only discourage male violence, but also encourage Women's violence against men. She says that when men fear retaliation their violence will stop. She talks about the need to make Women literate in the tools of violence. She even says that, by encouraging Women's violence against men, some men who have not yet attacked Women may become victims of violence too, but she says that this is still preferable to the current status quo of male violence. Attacking "innocent" men is femicide prevention. When a Woman is violent toward a man, she contributes to a social good by reducing male violence against Women. By attacking and instilling fear in a man, and potentially in other men as well, especially if the act is public, she ensures

greater safety for Women. The public nature of such an act can serve as a deterrent, making men more hesitant to engage in violence against Women.

A Woman has the right to exploit and use a man, as men collectively owe reparations for the generations of free labor they have extracted from Women. If a Woman terrorizes a man and forces him into unpaid labor, she is simply enacting justice by reclaiming what was unjustly taken from Women in the past. Women are entitled to their own spaces, privacy, and the autonomy to decide how they structure their environments. However, they should also have unrestricted access to any space they choose, as there should be no areas designated exclusively for men.

Women should have complete control over reproduction and the future of the species, determining which men are allowed to reproduce and which should be sterilized, ensuring the extinction of certain genetic lines. Every act of violence committed by a Woman against a man is an act of resistance and liberation, as the oppressed always have the right to use violence against their oppressors.

In a nutshell, feminism is supposed to be everything they accuse you of being and you keep denying that it is. They keep accusing you of being a violent misandrist because they know their crimes are so vile, an evil misandrist is exactly who they deserve. You don't see your own potential yet your mere awareness of an unjust system is striking fear in their guilty hearts.

Multiple times in the book I've said that every man believes that he's born to rule the world, but this quote is incomplete. The complete quote is "every man believes that he's born to rule the world, and until you can physically kick the shit out of him, it's going to stay this way." But this quote is again, incomplete. When we say 'you' who exactly

are we talking to? And kick him where?

A man getting beat up by another man wouldn't hurt him the way getting humiliated by a Woman would. For a man, his ego is very important, his ego is what is running him. Until a Woman can crush his ego with the minimal efforts, the man will worship this layer of narcissism he's created around his heart.

Males fight all the time, just to be trained in fighting. Losing to another male is just another day because it becomes a matter of skill, and skills can be gained or improved. But losing to a Woman because she... kicked you in the balls? There's nothing you can do about it. She won because you are a male and she is a Woman, and there is nothing you can do to change that. She expressed her superiority over your body, on your body. She used what makes you male to defeat you. She didn't necessarily out-skill you, or outmaneuver you, or overpowered you, she was just a Woman that knew being a male makes you weak. That inescapable inferiority is what gets to your ego.

When a man gets beat up or loses from a man, it's just another defeat in the dick swinging competition, like okay, we went to war and lost, no big deal. He dusts his shirt off and moves on.

But when a Woman hurts a man's ego it drives him insane. But just breaking his ego isn't enough. He must be beaten and humiliated both physically and verbally to have his ego crushed.

As a content creator on YouTube, I post videos verbally humiliating men. I do tag them femdom, but I'm not saying anything a normal dominatrix would say.

If you look at "professional dominatrix" and their content, they "humiliate" men by calling them sissy or your dick is so small it looks like a clit or you should dress like

a Woman you're not a real man. Who exactly is being humiliated here? So far, she only humiliated Women. And there are all the sultry and sexy voices like "yeah, I would hurt you really good, so you like when I hurt you?" How is this dominance? You are clearly trying to please him.

Besides, dominatrixes often have the most sexist patriarchal views and reproduce a lot of alpha-real men content "you're inferior, but REAL men are superior". But I am telling men that you're inferior because you're a man.

Femdom is just male supremacy and porn.

So, expecting a sultry voice telling them that they're a Woman because they're not "man enough" these, pornheads would click on my videos. A lot of times, I'd prove to be even 'too much' for the males who extract pleasure out of degradation. First, they'd leave comments saying "goddess you're absolutely right, men are useless and unworthy" and a few seconds later they'd start explaining how the downfall of the civilization isn't completely men's fault, Women contributed equally to the downfall. Some would question where exactly is the humiliation? All I would talk about is the male psychology and how they're nothing but monkeys with a sword. They would be terrified to encounter me, an actual dominant Woman who genuinely enjoys seeing men in pain and is aware that she is superior and males are inferior.

The reason why men like femdom in the first place is because men are naturally submissive. They seek to submit. But the patriarchal molding process which both Women and men are subjected to, doesn't even leave a tiny scope for us to consider that it's actually the male who is subordinate to the Woman. Men don't understand this, but I do, and I mentally fried multiple men through this. One day, I found my Patreon spammed with comments and likes by a male.

To protect his identity, let's call him Male. Male belongs to a high stratum from the Dickerarchy, this information also plays an important role in understanding how his mind works. So, while I was under the covers in my room, Male spammed by likes and comments, his comments were long and he talked about how much he liked my videos. I am used to being complimented like this, but Male's comments were different.

The point of sharing this incident isn't to talk about how influential I am, that's already established, but to show you what I mean when I say men need to be tamed. Everything I said in this book will sting men to the deepest and entertain Women to their core. Why is that? I understand men and the male psychology deeply, other Women do too, but they've buried these observations deep inside, I am basically tickling that part.

"I used to train kickboxing while ago. Got beaten up during sparings many times which helped me improve my fighting skills. Honestly, You made me feel beaten the same way. It was not sexual type of arousal. You just got in to my head and made me feel humbled and defeated. You have very strong aura."

Every man believes that he's born to rule the world, and until a Woman can physically kick the shit out of him, it's going to stay this way. I never met Male in real life, never got the chance to physically attack his balls. The videos that I post on my channel are nothing less than a constant verbal degradation of men. Why do I post them? To show and make men come face to face with the deepest judgements they have of themselves that they've been running away from.

Men normally get triggered really bad upon criticism by Women. Why is that? It's because deep down they know the criticism is true and the fact that a superior being is

saying this, they start fearing for their lives. Men know they deserve the worst for all their crimes against Womanity. I, on the other hand, am putting it all out there. Every bit of evil the man has done is being not only talked about but also criticized by someone they fear.

Men react to criticism in three ways:

a. They will either get highly triggered and angry, and will get the urge to hurt you physically. Typical male behavior.

b. He will experience sexual arousal. His biggest fear is ceasing to exist, so, his brain sexualizes this fear to protect itself. His brain, much like his balls, acts against him. He will jerk off to it. His arousal comes from the hormones produced in his balls, which is ironic considering that balls get even more sensitive to attack during arousal. It's like balls are suicidal somehow.

c. Accept what I am saying as he realizes that most of his anger induced from my speech is just ego triggers. He lets me break his ego and does not bother fighting back. It's not like there is any desire left to fight anymore after the ego is broken anyway.

The third one tends to be much more common than you would expect. However, it is the most common in men coming from a higher stratum of the Dickerarchy. Everything I say about men isn't only what I think about them, it's also what men think about themselves.

"First I felt triggered by Your words and aroused by Your personality. I was looking in Your eyes and wondering if I would be able to maintain eye contact while talking to You in reality. I felt pressure in my stomach and throat"

The stomach is where the *Manipur Chakra*, which is the center of personal power, is located. I triggered his powerlessness with my words, hence the pressure. The

throat has the *Vishuddhi Chakra* which triggered his inability to defend himself. He felt powerless in front of me.

"My subconsciousness mind started to tell me „forget Your ego, she is right". That was very stressfull day for me, but somehow I relaxed just laying in dark room without any censor stimulation, just listening to Your voice. It was somehow therapeutical...

Like freeing myself from ego made me feel better. Usually I hate myself after this type of thoughts

This time I felt relaxed, my performance next day was better and in the evening I thought „lets listen to her again"

The most important point here is, why did it feel therapeutical to him? Why did he feel better after I "defeated" him?

He felt like, for once, that he can "be himself", that he can be submissive. A man's true nature is submission. He saw that a 'leader' is around. The same leader that no one in his entire life ever mentioned to him before. A Woman leading and the man submitting? That's something totally new, something that wouldn't make it outside the bedroom. Someone claiming that the natural order is men submitting to Women and Women leading the society with absolutely no fear and hesitation? He never heard of something like that ever before but his subconscious lit up when he heard me. No matter who you think you are consciously, or who you claim to be consciously, is irrelevant, you're nothing more than the result of your subconscious beliefs and you're ran by your subconscious programming, and as I like to say "You're not in control". We already saw that in the example of a non-empowered Woman becoming a feminist.

There is this realization that you are finally in tune with nature. You've been trying to be this thing you were clearly not made to do, but now you can finally live a life as nature

intended for your kind to live, and you will feel that this is the just, natural, logical way to live and to see Women above you.

I, a Woman, am telling men that they're way below me because they're naturally incompetent and the only thing they should be focused on is slaving away for Women. His true nature found an opportunity to reveal itself. His subconscious mind saw that, and my videos brought him closer to his true nature which is to submit to a Woman. I broke him so hard that I fixed him.

What separates a patriarchal man and a submissive man? His ego. My words broke that ego barrier which let his true nature of submission reveal itself. The aim of your ego is to destroy you, yet you spend your entire life trying to protect it. Let it break. Every trigger you feel is a chance for your ego to break. But instead of letting the fire of Power break your ego, you react. Instead of observing your triggers you react with angry outbursts. Your reaction is an attempt to keep that ego alive. Your trigger is the fire cremating your ego.

When I broke his ego, I relieved him. I relieved Male. He felt relieved because the illusion of his ego was destroyed to a certain extent by me. *Your ego is a burden on your mind. You're constantly wasting your energy trying to protect something which is literally existing to destroy you. Much like trying to protect your balls which are slowly killing you.*

In the book Eve: How the Female Body Drove 200 million Years of Human Evolution, which looks at evolution through the POV of Women, the author talks about how balls make men live less, and she says "if you want to make males live longer, there is an easy solution to that, cut the balls off." and then presents some studies of how castrated male animals live on average longer than ball-having ones.

I did not defeat him; I defeated his ego. His biggest enemy was killed by me.

"No. I have never sent money online to anyone after self-destroying my ego with her speeches. Don't know how You got me here, but I just submitted myself. I thought at first "pick the first tier for, what if this is a scam" - but I just did what I felt i Have to."

My Patreon has four tiers, $10, $20, $50, $100. He picked the most expensive one. He does not know why he did that but I do. He was in his submissive zone. He was seeking submission. He 'submitted' his money to me because he knows 'leader' knows better. That was his subconscious working, not his conscious.

This is why we think that men "provide". They're not giving the Woman money because 'I'm the great king and she's subordinate to me', remember how men seek power to further exploit and not serve, but because 'leader knows better'. They submit their wealth to the leader.

Pay attention to the fact that he's never sent money to anyone online. But he did to me after I destroyed his ego. His ego stopped him from submitting, so I destroyed it and he submitted. Hence, he was tamed. "Don't know how you got me here" but I know that perfectly.

"Me saying,"scrote, you literally carry the proof of your inferiority between your legs, a slight flick will send you into multiple rounds of pain" would break your male ego" I said.

"Hurts. Just reading. My voice would shake if I was about to reply on that" He replied

His voice would shake responding to a verbal attack of testicular terrorism. This man is 29-year-old millionaire, yet his voice would shake trying to respond to a 22-year-old university student with no job. No matter how many accolades a man has, he will always suffer from an

inferiority complex especially when it comes to dealing with Women. The only reason why men get to be in power is because Women overestimate men and underestimate themselves. I bet when a pick-me is agreeing with men's garbage, even the men get confused.

Women are the ones who truly believe in the myth of male supremacy, whereas men fully understand that it is nothing more than a falsehood. However, rather than admitting this, they deliberately deceive Women and uphold the illusion. In reality, it is Women who internalize and sustain this belief, while men must constantly exert effort, engage in labor, and maintain a façade to keep the illusion of male supremacy alive. Without these continuous efforts, the entire construct would collapse, revealing the truth that male dominance is nothing more than a carefully maintained deception.

"Oh, yeah. Balls as manifestation of male inferiority – that part got me as hell. I felt little afraid while listening to that"

As I said before, Women overestimate men. Men are constantly in a self-defense mode, and Women finding out that balls are the most sensitive organ on their body that can make them feel pain of weeks, would terrify them.

In my career as an online male bully, I have tried multiple tactics to defeat the male, those tactics do work, but ever since I've discovered about the male weakness balls and started using verbal **Testicular Terrorism** to terrify the male, for the first time in my life am I finding it so easy to defeat men. Men would either block me, change their tone, or gaslight me into thinking that it doesn't hurt that much.

But it does. Balls are the proof of the male weakness which they carry between their legs. Thats why I call it the I-hate-being-a-man package.

Men have a raging fear of getting their balls attacked. Use it or exploit it. Male felt afraid because his 'secret' that he's actually very weak and easy to defeat is out.

"Your balls is your weakness and I know that lol" I replied

"Yes they are... But you hurt them even without kicking. And I am somehow grateful. Never felt that way." Responded Male

What terrifies and degrades men to their core is

a. Reminding them that balls make them weak, inferior, and subject to intense pain

b. That you know that

c. That you are willing to hurt balls, knowing the traumatic pain and loss of self-confidence it will bring, and that you will enjoy it

Like imagine, a male expressing how much he would suffer if you hit his balls, expecting he would get sympathy, but instead it's you just laughing and saying "that's so funny, can I cause you that suffering? I really want to see for myself."

He's hurt because his little secret is out. His biggest insecurity is being made fun of openly. Men are insecure about their balls that's why they tried so hard to change the narrative around them. Associating balls with power and authority.

There is a different between making fun of his stupid hairstyle, or his balding, and to make fun of his ball pain. I think what horrifies males in a way when they hear the laughter or notice the smiles and the joy from Women, is a kind of loneliness in pain that I'm the only one feeling bad here, but feeling bad makes them happy. I'm in so much pain and they don't care, they are not worried, they are not concerned. Like, sometimes I see videos of accidental hits to the nuts and the Woman is trying to say sorry but she can't complete the sentence because she can't stop laughing so much at him. I

think in a way that is a moment when males deal with their spend-ability. They don't matter, their pain doesn't matter, their suffering doesn't matter, Girls are jumping for joy and high-fiving each other, your suffering is entertainment to them.

Men, including Male, have told me that I'm sadistic for finding joy in men's testicular pain. This is just another way for men to feel powerful even during their suffering. They still cannot accept that the patriarchy in reality being so fragile IS hilarious. It's not only hilarious because of how pathetic men look whimpering in pain caused by the slightest effort on your part, but you're also laughing out of joy that comes from feeling free of that patriarchal brainwashing that kept you in fear for so long, only to realize what a joke it is to say males are superior and stronger while they were carrying balls all along, that the very symbol of their 'strength' is their greatest weakness. Men start to look like a joke. Their superiority starts to look like a lie, because that's what it is. Male superiority is an oxymoron. **Testicular Terrorism** has given 'fragile masculinity' a whole new meaning.

It got me thinking on the difference in terms of the psychological damage caused as well. A Girl going "Oh, I'm so sorry, I didn't mean it, are you okay?" and a Girl laughing at you and rubbing salt in the wound and showing that she not only isn't sorry, but she feels great about it.

The realization that this isn't over. If a Girl apologizes and feel bad and cares for your pain, it's like your brain is telling you "Well, this feels painful but she won't do it again anymore, we're safe after this". But to see how happy she got by doing it, it's like she is telling you "This was fun, I might have to do it again". The agony won't end there, at any other point in time she might remind you of how painful it feels, and how much she likes that

it feels that way."

Just like Vira, I was too subjected to a patriarchal brainwashing where I was told to not only see the male humans as the epitome of power, authority, strength, and dominance, but also see myself as a dependent, weak, and a fragile being surviving at the mercy of males. Just to end up discovering that the entire veneer of bravado that males carry is made of cotton, all I have to do is lift a knee to make my way.

But why was Male grateful? He felt grateful because he felt lighter after I freed him from his own ego and his belief that a Woman can never humiliate a male, even if she's better than him she must be humble in front of him to protect his ego. I, on the other hand, an unemployed university student from a third world country, said the truth about the inferiority of this 29-year-old millionaire sitting in Europe without hesitating. Only Women have the ability to break a man's ego.

You see Women being superior to you all the time, but before, this caused you some cognitive dissonance, even anger, "how dare she be better than me, doesn't she know her place?"

Then, you realize, it was I who did not know my place, it all makes sense now.

Did he realize that he was tamed?

"At first I was very skeptical but somehow You got more convincing with every word. I felt intrigued to even argue or debate You cuz I also love debates (lawyer by education) but I also get ego-motivated during them. I was "afraid" of going into arguments right away cuz this is what usually do, and then I stand my ground till end like psycho-autist till the end I extracted great value from You thanks to putting my ego aside,

that was really mindblowing and I think I'm gonna be "Yes Mam" type of a guy for a while."

Triggers are an assassination attempt on your ego. As mentioned before, Male did get triggered and had the urge to debate me where he would stand his ground even if the ground is swallowing him inside, but Male did not do that because of his high status in the Dickerarchy. Male feels safer as compared to his Beta counterparts, he did see me as a threat but not enough where his mental emergency alarms would set off. Male is safer as compared to his non-millionaire counterparts, but Male is a male, his ontological insecurities are still there. If Male belonged to a lower stratum of the Dickerarchy, or worse, suffered from a Beta Male Complex, he wouldn't be on my Patreon, but in my YouTube comments telling me how he's going to find me and teach me a lesson or two on feminism. But since Male's ontological inferiority was covered by his millionaire and racial status, he let his triggers take his ego out and bring him closer to his natural state.

"I felt that way only because I discovered some kind of mental strenght in You. You are braver than me in a sense, that I would never go for a war with all world same way as You are doing. That impressed me."

I know.

"22 year old Girl broke my ego despite that

Yes, You are very good in argumentation

Most of my counterpoints would be stripped down to ego triggers"

Ego triggers. Ego forms where there is a lack of love.

"There might some young boys that might turn to redpill or other crap after hearing You. U consider it a statistic, but still, Your content is recycled by Your enemies, not the best method of doing war" said Male

"Tbh a real enemy would be another Woman who's defending men. I can't see men as enemies. They look like untamed wild horses and dogs. Why would I be angry at an animal for being true to its nature." I replied

"Feeling pressure in my throat and stomach reading this is normal reaction amongst men? Trying to trigger me?" Said Male

You'd be shocked. They only react violently to me online, in real life during face-to-face conversations, they can't even maintain an eye contact.

"Like I had this mental barrier and it's gone"

Mental barrier of ego, and it's gone because I kicked its balls.

Just my words alone were powerful enough for this XY to be tamed. But Male belongs to the higher stratum of the Manosphere, those belonging to the lower strata might be harder to tame through verbal **Testicular Terrorism**, and those suffering from a Beta Male Complex will seek pleasure in any form of Female interaction.

Then what is the solution? Everyone always told me that I, as a Woman, am physically weaker than males, so how will I ever tame and control males?

Nature did not create Women physically weaker. Even though, over centuries, your frame became smaller than the average man's due to men subjecting you to artificial undernourishment, it still doesn't change the fact that he's carrying two discipline tools between his legs. That sad sack is a sort of weapon from the Ultimate Matriarch to the Womanity, the one that men have but belongs to Women, because she knew what she was creating.

This is yet another projection by males against Women. One of the main reasons why Women became smaller than males on average is because of undernourishment.

Basically, telling Women to go on diets, eat just salads, eat little, eat only after the males finished, etc. Since the male undernourishment is real, they created artificial man-made undernourishment on Women to compensate for their own natural inferiority.

Also have you ever tried training and getting self-defense classes? Toughen up, you can easily defeat a male.

We have often been told that violence is evil, and that peace and love are the solution to all world problems, and they're absolutely right! It's my love for Women, Girls, animals, cars, and McChicken sandwiches which inspired this divine solution: **Testicular Terrorism**: the ultimate end to male violence against Women.

We have been told that violence is evil by man, the same man who has every interest in keeping Women pacified, while they themselves never follow their own advice and keep being violent.

Violence is evil is what you teach slaves so that they don't revolt against your oppressive rule over them. But then he goes around teaching his own son that violence is needed to maintain power and rule over others.

Agony, distress, and pain are requirements of the training process. You can't tame a wild horse without showing it the fear of consequences. You can't teach it right from wrong because it simply doesn't have the ability to understand it. You need to not tell, but show it what would happen if the horse did something that its master does not approve of, it will be whipped.

A lot of male entitlement comes from being able to get away with their insolence to the Womankind. So, to show them consequences is the best way to end it.

Similarly, if an XY chooses to let his animalistic instincts run wild as a horse, the patriarchy will be kicked out of him through the **Bag of Pain**, dangling precariously where a Woman's **Portal of Life** stands, between the legs.

The agony and distress men experienced when I told them, while sitting on OmeTV, that the two rubber balls in my hands were their balls and that I would bust them was all I needed to understand how to tame a male. The denial of pain, the rejection of their own vulnerability, and the sheer embarrassment, I could already see a victim in their eyes. They said, "No it doesn't hurt that much" but would say no when I'd ask them to kick their own balls then.

It is important to start kicking men in their nuts right from their childhood. Training of a dog starts when he's a puppy, training of men also starts when they're boys. Little Girls should be taught that you should aim for a male's nuts if he's annoying you, disturbing you, or if they're bored. It doesn't get more traumatizing than knowing literally any Woman or Girl you see on the streets could just decide to kick you regardless of what you did. You just wanted to go buy some milk, but met a Girl, and came back home with an omelet as well.

This has an important effect on Girls too. Every Woman that had experienced kicking balls from an early age, grew up to have such exhilarating confidence and self-love, and none of them treat males as if they're Gods or as creatures to be feared. They were also all smart and accomplished people, probably because it allows them to put themselves first and focus on themselves rather than pleasing boys and seeking their validation. Little boys should become victims of **Testicular Terrorism** to keep them in check right from their childhood.

Everything you create becomes your property, and since Women create men, men are also Women's properties.

When a man becomes the victim of **Testicular Terrorism**, it's a lesson in humility. The agony radiates through his body, rendering him powerlessness, with its impact lingering far beyond the initial shock. It instills a deep, almost primal fear, an awareness that his most fragile weakness is exposed, hanging between his legs like a built-in system of accountability.

"It's such a well-designed system of discipline to make you aware of your own powerlessness, it literally removes all your power, you have no strength, your organs don't function well, your brain is gone, you lose all control. It's an empirical taste of full and complete powerlessness at the hands of a Woman." - victim of **Testicular Terrorism.**

*This reminds me of Freud's theories of castration anxiety, that part of the male development stage is fear of castration. It is there in his brain, just waiting to be awakened. You are awakening this primal fear that is already in their brains. Their brains were built-in with a function to be subjected to **Testicular Terrorism**, just goes on to say that balls are there for Women to use.*

From that moment on, he moves through the world with caution, second-guessing any impulse to disrespect or harm a Woman. After all, he has learned that his discipline tools are not in his hands, but rather, within an easy reach of those he might seek to oppress.

Men who have endured **Testicular Terrorism** often develop an unspoken reverence for Women, not just because of the pain inflicted but because of the symbolic power behind it. With each well-placed kick, it is not just flesh that is struck, but an entire system of entitlement. In that fleeting moment of devastation, the patriarchy itself

trembles.

There are also some studies which suggest that men with bigger balls are more aggressive and worse fathers. Men who excel in nurturing and child-rearing tend to have smaller balls, while men with bigger balls don't, as they produce too much testosterone, making them more aggressive, less likely to settle down, more prone to cheating, and abandoning their families. Interestingly, bigger balls also mean bigger ball pain.

So, if you're wondering whether a man would actually castrate himself to get revenge on you, so you couldn't attack his balls, then no, it's not happening. With the loss of his balls, his testosterone and aggression would die too.

That's why Women should be **Testicular Terrorists**. Don't wait for a male to be disobedient. Don't wait to sacrifice some unknown poor Woman, baby, or goat for you to punish him, also why would you at this point? Subject males to both physical and verbal **Testicular Terrorism** as much as you can. It's not only a training for men but also for you, to realize and experience first-hand the power that the Great Mother gave you. Men are afraid of having their balls smashed, so talk about it as much as you can. Be in public with your Girlfriends and talk about how you punched a guy's nuts because he was looking at you the wrong way, or because he didn't at all, he was just there and that you felt like it. Go and randomly smash one or two pair as well, gesture them randomly that you will attack them there. **Testicular terrorism** can end male violence against Women and hence dismantle the patriarchy.

A lot of male entitlement comes from this belief that ultimately, he can take her by force and she won't resist. If you show him that he has no force and is physically at her mercy, then all entitlement will be gone. Not only that, but

he will begin to understand that She is entitled to decide what happens to him.

Men possess a natural aggression fueled by testosterone, a raw force that, if properly directed, can be transformed into disciplined energy. Women, being natural born leaders, must tame the male into using his aggression smartly. But, do Women need men's force?

Women have plenty of strength, and especially if all the patriarchal system of keeping Women small and weak is gone, then Women's natural body strength would also be restored. So, what is the function of males? Their strength only appears as useful because he robbed Women's strength.

And why must the system by lead by Women? I mean Women aren't free therapies or construction workers for men, so why can't men train each other after receiving a singular training from Women?

Would you trust men to self-educate and educate each other?

The education system for males should be overseen by Women, instilling discipline, appropriate fear, and rigorous spiritual training. Male-only spaces must be completely abolished, if they can barely conduct themselves in public, what chaos would they create in isolation? Do we let dogs run free in shelters or in doggy daycare? No, they are governed by humans. In a man's day care it won't be any different either.

But before that, the male population is also supposed to go lower. The male population is not supposed to be this high. If it was not for the constant Female feticide and infanticide, and male violence against Women, we would not have these many men. In India and China, we have 70

million extra men. They're extra with no need for them to exist. It is these useless men that go around in their sad lonely "mommy didn't love me enough" groups in India creating men's rights movements and meninism to get men the rights that Women took from men under patriarchy.

Patri·archy

['peɪtrɪɑːki]

noun

a system of society or government in which the father or eldest male is head of the family and descent is reckoned through the male line.

This is peak incompetence. After thousands of years of patriarchy, if you still need men's right movements, then just give up. What kind of a superior being ends up oppressing itself in a system it created to apparently benefit only itself?

When males took power through physical and psychological warfare, and bloodshed, and installed a patriarchy, the first thing they did was come out with ways to erase Women-only spaces and to separate Women from each other. They made the nuclear family so Women were isolated from other Women and into a male's house. The beginning of Feminism is precisely when this was first broken, and Women could meet each other in factories, for instance, and they start talking to each other and realizing they have a common problem in men. Then they unite and fight.

Even social media has been one such catalyst. On social media, Women don't physically meet each other, but an exchange of ideas and problems is involved. Women come together, teach and learn from each other. Social media is playing a huge role in the transition into the Matriarchy.

After failing to force Women back into isolation, men have struggled to contain Women's connections with each other. Yet, they persist. Enforcing radically misogynistic censorship systems that allow pages openly defending rape while removing content for something as simple as saying, 'men are trash'.

Besides, learning discipline from another male is nothing like learning your place below a Woman superior to you. You don't fear another man, you just bide your time until you can defeat him. But with Women? You can't defeat her.

There's a difference between dogs competing for the alpha status, and a dog's reverence to humans. A male is a male, if he loses to another male, it's just a setback, but he is not inferior to that male, he just lost. But he can win. Males are used to watching big comebacks from boxing, MMA, or sports in general, that teaches them the heroism of getting up and trying again.

But when it is a Woman who defeats him using his manhood, then he learns he can't get back up. There's no training in the world that can bring him even remotely close to her. He lost the moment his balls dropped.

As the physical embodiments of the Mother Nature, we honor all her creations no matter how wild they seem to be. Men have fire within them to create and achieve, they just need to be tamed and trained on how to channel them resourcefully. But why teach men when you can teach Women instead? Women can achieve much more than men can, why waste resources on something lesser when you have plenty of Women in need of attention and resources and knowledge, etc.

Men are the support system of Women. Men must submit to the Matriarchs and follow her instructions. His

divine goal is to serve her. That's why he's created. Any male caught in an act of disobedience is a huge liability. He is no longer needed on the planet. A man's job is to do the work that Women don't want to, or any work that Women assign him to do. Femininity is the being, and masculinity is the action created by the Femininity. The being can exist without actions but there's no actions without the being existing itself. A man's life aim is to serve the Womanity and Mother Nature, for it, he can even be sacrificed.

Yes, all men, every single one. Every single person who has a pair hanging between their legs should have their ballginity broken at a young age by getting kicked there. Men in their natural state are animalistic, and an animal's training starts right from its childhood. It's important to make all them go through this experience. It's almost like a ritual, a rite of passage, how boys learn what being a male means and what it entails. Men need to be tamed; balls are just where we start.

The day Women start randomly attacking men on their balls, unprovoked, is the day when rape stats will fall, when men will truly learn to behave. Love can fix the world, so learn to love Women. That's how you get every male to fear every Woman, that's how you give them the fear that there is no escaping this, it's just a matter of when, not if they will be kicked.

You should never feel ashamed or guilty about kicking men in the balls, you should enjoy it. Men have always proven through their words and actions how they truly believe that our body is their choice. But the worst part is that, they're not doing something good with the control that they gain. I don't think any person would mind someone else taking care of their needs and making decisions on their behalf, but the decisions that men make has always

proven to be nothing more than an act of selfishness. Time and time again men have shown that their only aim is to gain as much control as possible over Women. They want to control Women, their children, nature, and all natural resources.

As natural born leaders, it's onto Women to decide what happens with her property, not the property itself. The property itself is incapable of thinking beyond itself. Women have to step up for the sake of the safety of their children and pets and realize that his body is indeed her choice.

When you kick a man in his balls, you're doing the world a favor. You're making sure that this particular man will find it unthinkable to disrespect or harass any other Woman, because he is now enlightened that he has two torture devices attached to his body. You should not wait for a man to do something bad or display symptoms of savagery in order to punish him.

Every day that the patriarchy has not seized to exist, a male is guilty of not ending it, so he already deserves it anyway.

When a Woman is raped, it keeps all other Women oppressed. It lets Women know what would happen if she dared leave her house, or practice her right to choose, or chose to exist, since most rapes happen to Women by men they know inside their homes.

So, similarly, when you strike this barbarian in his testicles, you let it know what could happen if he dares savagery to take over his brain. You're not only putting the victim of **Testicular Terrorism** in check, you're also keeping the men who witnessed this act of terrorism in check.

Kick him, kick him full force. This won't be a light playful kick, no, this will carry the collective rage of Women for

centuries of oppression, taking the rightful vengeance in your precariously perched appendage, causing such a crushing force that instant rupture is a fair possibility. Then, tell us how much you like it between one bout of vomiting nausea to the next.

In the end, don't believe me blindly. Test it out for yourself. Kick a pair.

(T.T) *The symbol of **Testicular Terrorism**. The male tears shaping into two T's.*

In conclusion, we hit them where it hurts physically and mentally. Why exactly do you think that the Ultimate Matriarch didn't bother giving men any protection around their balls, and put them at a kickable height for both, the Woman's knee and her fist? Because when She made man, She knew what She was doing. She gave the world men to serve it. But then we slowly descended into the age of Darkness.

V
The Age of Pisces

"This struggle of the human Female toward sex equality will end in a new sex order, with the Female as superior."- Nikola Tesla

It can't really be proven with our beloved science and statistics because intuition and spirituality are looked down upon under patriarchy, but they are real, very real. All Women are blessed with an inbuilt Female instinct. The Female instinct is like the 99% material of the Y chromosome, it is there but never gets used. The main reason why Women tend to convince themselves to ignore their instincts and do as other people are coercing them to do is because Women are kept ignorant of the immense powers and abilities they naturally possess. I mean, in order to acknowledge that Women are powerful spiritually, you'd have to admit that they have something on men, that somewhere, they stand above males. Although they stand above males in every possible aspect, if they started praising you for your inbuilt spiritual qualities, they'd be reminded of how there's no such thing as a male instinct since men are closer to death and Women are closer to life.

Additionally, we are told to "rest in our Feminine and let the man lead", which is just the rebranding of "Women are stupid and shouldn't use their brains", the only time you, *as a Woman*, should want to *"rest in your Feminine while a man protects and provides"* is when you're dealing with men in relationships. No, you don't actually believe in it, you're just exploiting misogyny for your own benefit.You underestimate yourself and trust the male decision making, not knowing that the male only thinks of himself. Lastly, Women are made to feel evil and wretched for centering and prioritizing themselves. Of course, patriarchy is all about exploiting and extracting.

Spiritually, the masculine and its over powering has been evil. The age of Pisces or the age of darkness is a time period staring 2000 years ago. This age is the age of Patriarchy. Spiritually it is believed that the patriarchy did not exist before this time, even if it did, it wasn't powerful or was just taking its baby steps. The age of darkness, as this patriarchal period is called, says that males will have dominion over the planet and will be in power. This period is scarce in divine Feminine energy. In this period, we will live in an unnatural order where men are the "leaders" or in the position of power, using the power to further exploit. The male population was also huge in this time period. *Who the hell needs these many sperm dispensers?!* Even the all-loving love-is-the-strongest-force spirituality has named the male-authority as dark.

The past 2000 years also saw the rise of abrahamic religions which attempted to divinify the male. Their God is a man. *Their God has balls, their God is weak.* A man as greedy, evil, and egoistic as our average male. Well, in that sense, man was created in the spitting image of their God; worship Him or get thrown into hellfire, how kind. Man could not

accept that Women create life so he created God, the same God that told us that Eve came from adam's rib.

The Great Mother religions, which flourished in ancient cultures across the globe, revered Mother Nature as the ultimate source of creation, fertility, and life. These traditions often centered on the worship of a Divine Feminine force, embodying both the nurturing aspects of life and the inevitable power of death and regeneration. Women were seen as the sacred manifestations of this duality, representing the entirety of creation and the cyclical nature of existence. In these societies, men often occupied a secondary role, serving as complements to the primary creative and destructive powers of the Feminine Divine. The Great Mother was not only a symbol of life-giving but also of the transformative forces of nature, reflecting a worldview where balance and harmony were maintained through the reverence of the Feminine principle.

In contrast, the abrahamic narrative of adam's rib creating Eve represents a significant departure from the Great Mother's traditions, seeking to invert the primacy of the Feminine in creation. By framing Eve as derived from adam, the story positions man as the original and Woman as the derivative, effectively subordinating the Feminine to the masculine. This narrative can be seen as an attempt to usurp the ancient reverence for the Great Mother and her role as the sole source of creation. The Christian for instance, took the matriarchal religion idea of Nymph, Mother, and Crone, made it Mary, the Virgin (Nymph) Mother, while the Crone, that symbolizes Women's wisdom and is the Matriarchal figure, became the Witch to be hunted. By placing men at the center of the origin story, the tale of adam's rib reinforces a patriarchal hierarchy,

diminishing the sacred status of Women and their connection to the life-giving and transformative powers of nature that were once universally celebrated. Later, in the Middle Ages they hunted the Midwifes and replaced them with male doctors, so that instead of the Mother - Woman being the life giver, the male doctor became the figure associated with bringing life into the world.

Keeping the religious psychosis aside, this age of Pisces is coming to an end. We are moving from the age of darkness to the age of light, as it is called by spiritualists. The upcoming age after the age of Pisces is called the age of Aquarius. From the word "light" you should be able to tell that one of its traits is that the world will go back to its natural order of the Matriarchy, where Women rightfully take up the position they were meant to take, as leaders. Women and Femininity are better than men and masculinity. So no, the world will not get worse, it is bound to improve. The patriarchy is dying, almost as if it is adding to the male suicide rates. No matter who does what, every step will lead to Women in power.

This age shift started as soon as the calendars changed from 1999 to 2000. It's like 2000 was the kick to the balls, and now we are just watching patriarchy slowly agonizing in pain as the result. If you pay attention, the previous millennium started from the number 1. In numerology, 1 is a masculine number. *1 is the loneliest number, which given the male loneliness epidemic, would make 1 very masculine indeed.* For a thousand years, the world experienced an amplified masculine energy, reinforced by both the dominance of 1 and the influence of the Age of Pisces. We witnessed multiple genocides, wars, colonization, famines, epidemics, pandemics, and of course femicide over and over again. Since the male thinks he is the center of the universe and

chosen by God, in simpler terms, that he's better than Women and that the best thing one could ever be is a man, he believes that a society full of wars, genocides, and oppression is peak development, because that's exactly what we saw after his kind took over. Yes, the male believes that such pain is inevitable. He will never admit that he is incapable of running countries, he will tell himself lies that *wars, rapes, and pedophilia are inevitable, so nothing ever is my fault.* For a man, he will only rise if someone else falls. Instead of expanding his own boundaries, he erases those of others.

Rape, pedophilia, bestiality, what low did men not reach? In 2024, my video telling men to kill themselves instead of raping Women went viral in MRA spaces, a man commented how they need to be eviler and stop being kind to Women.

There is a lot to unpack here. First off, men can be worse than raping babies? And secondly, what kindness? I mean if you're promoting men boycott Women, then I do support this men's 4B. Ignore Women, boycott us, act like we don't exist. But what exact kindness are you referring to? To stop the kindness, you would have had to be kind in the first place.

They have a name for it, MGTOW (Men Going Their Own Way).
Except that MGTOW men spend most of their times not leaving Women alone on the internet.

"Men built the civilization", is usually their replies. "Everything you see Vira, is built by men." He said with a spark in his eyes and a soft smile on his face. Taking credit for all the garbage on streets and the dying planet as if its peak human development. *"The winner of this competition is usually the one who has oppressed the most, the one who stole*

the most, and conquered the most. He might have killed the most, bought and sold the most, and as comes with the penis package, raped the most." This is also men's version of "love" and "kindness" towards Women. Men express "love" and devotion through acts of service naturally as submission and servitude is their true nature. Though their services require Women's order and desire which has lately been missing.

Do males even realize why exactly it was men who "built the civilization," and not Women? Men did not build the civilization because our delicate Feminine arms gave up on us as we were laying bricks, and we begged the males to come to our rescue, no, this isn't what happened. Through physical and psychological warfare, you tied Women inside homes, you burnt Women at stake, had them married off as little Girls, you raped and burnt unmarried Women alive. It was you who told Women through religious brainwashing that a Woman's divine duty is to be in the kitchen and serve her husband, and the ones who dared disagree were called a Witch and burnt at stake. In simpler terms, Women had no freedom. They were commodities and properties passed on from one man to another. She was not a person of her own ever during this period.

You did not "build the civilization" because Women tried and failed, you "built the civilization" because there was only one person able to participate in its building, the male. Men spent centuries convincing Women that Women's happiness lies in the kitchen, just to turn around and taunt them that they contributed nothing, that they sat at homes while "men built the civilization." It's just another tactic by the insecure male to feel powerful. Man had to tie up Women inside their homes because the only time a man can win against a Woman is when Women refuse to show up for

the fight.

But even after all that, men still didn't build the civilization.

The idea of civilization only became possible due to the agricultural revolution. Who discovered agriculture? Women. So, Women's discovery and contributions to humanity are the basis of every civilization that ever existed. What men actually did was that they ruined civilizations. What men did was destroyed civilizations. How many civilizations were destroyed by men compared to how many they even claim to have created?" Replied Vira, kicking his balls even without touching them.

Women are life and males are death. That's why when a Woman kills a male, she is not death, but life, since she kills him so that Women can live.

But even then, Women did contribute to men's sad civilization through their unpaid labor as housewives. We all know that housewives work way more than corporate slaves with zero days off and no promotions. The work of housewives is only acknowledged and appreciated by feminists. It wasn't feminists who turned "make me a sandwich" and "back to the kitchen" into insults, it was men, the same men who still try to convince Women that their happiness lies in serving their husbands. You see how men have zero principles?

Though being a housewife generally puts women in an oppressive role, as she is dependent on the man for resources and has no power of her own in the real world, housewives can still be feminists and feminists can be housewives.

Housewife is a role created by the patriarchy to domesticate Women and its inherently anti-liberation. It also implies that marriage is natural and not a product of the patriarchal order to guarantee access of Women to men. But at the same time, any Woman can be a feminist, so that will include Women in any role, including some of the most oppressed among all: the housewife. If housewives, prostituted Women, and other deeply victimized Women can't be feminists, then who is feminism for?

The idea of housewives started only in the transition from Feudalism to Capitalism. Women were much more active in social life before they were pushed inside homes and away from the city.

The past thousand years saw the worst of the man. Women were given generational traumas because of men.

The past thousand years were masculine, and the current years are Feminine. Now the years start from the number 2. 2 is the Queen's number and its ruling planet, as called in numerology, is the Moon. This transition is not sudden as we still witness femicides all over the planet, it is said that the age of light will shine brighter from 2028 onward. As the people carrying the darkness of the 1900s keep dying, and as their children indoctrinate with their dark energy die too, the vibrations of the planet will increase.

In the recent years we witnessed a lot of deaths. The planet is changing its frequency and the Feminine energy is once again awakening on the planet as more and more humans with number 2 in their Lo-Shu grids populate the planet. We all must've heard that the earth was supposed to end in 2016, it did. That was the year when the divine Feminine started to breath once again. Her corpse experienced the flow of fresh air once again. That was the

year when she took her first breath after years of being buried. You can bury her, but you can never kill her. The year 2016 2+0+1+6 adds up to a 9. 9 is the number of end of cycles. The cycle of the curse on the Feminine ended that year. As I write this book in 2025, this year of 9 is also ending multiple cycles all over the world. I hope my book also ends the cycle of male superiority in your life.

The frequency of the planet is changing. It is increasing, and whoever fails to increase their frequency with it is eliminated from the planet. A lot of men died, my dad, my grandfather, my XY cousin, and one of my uncles. This is the time of spirituality and Femininity making its way back into our reality and whoever stays in the old patriarchal way of penis worship will be eliminated too. His body simply won't be able to exist in a divine environment. Like attracts like, and his like will attract a different reality. With the Queen's number 2, Femininity will govern the Earth once again.

In other words, fear will switch sides. *Energy can neither be created nor destroyed; rather, it can only be transformed or transferred from one form to another.*

This makes me question, is masculinity inherently evil? Why is the age of Femininity the age of light, and the age of masculinity is the age of darkness?

Andrew Tate, his destiny number, life path number, and name number, are all 1, according to numerology. I do not have to utter one word on how evil he is. This man is infused with the "divine" masculine energy as some call it, but not an inch of his body is divine. He's as divine as the hair on his head. That is because masculine energy is inherently evil.

And yours truly, Safa Hussain, is ruled by 2. I am ruled by 2 which is the Queen's number and my ruling planet is

the moon. My life path number being 9 which makes me a natural humanitarian giving me a natural desire to serve the Womanity, and astrologically me being ruled by Venus, infusing in me more Feminine energy. My birth name number, not my pen name, being at 6 or Venus, Feminine energy blessing me again and time of birth being 2:25 PM giving me the Feminine-Queen-Moon energy once again.

The fact that I am writing this book and openly talking about the Female superiority over the male is also a sign of the age transitioning from a patriarchy to a Matriarchy. Let the truth reveal itself to Womanity. Spirituality helped me refine my inner superior being energy, and carve myself into the very authentic Matriarch you witness today. This led me to create this Deprograming book for Women, to further help other Matriarchs channel the Mother Nature through them.

Giving men power and authority under the age of Pisces has led to them commit heinous crimes against Womanity which can never be forgiven. The crimes they committed because of an inherent inferiority complex that they carry within themselves, shows that men cannot lead as they don't exist beyond themselves.

The weight of these actions has created a massive collective karmic debt that men carry toward Women. History might not have recorded every act of misogyny, but the Akashic records have. Every injustice, every act of violence, it's all there, remembered by the universe even if humans choose to forget or pretend that they did not happen.

And this debt will be paid. Whether it happens through social change, personal accountability, or karmic consequences, the damage done will not go unanswered. Men will face the consequences for their actions, and the

pain Women have been put through get justice.

I could go on and on about the various injustices that the male kind put the Womanity through. Sati system, Salem Witch Trials, Female infanticide, Female feticide, pedophilia, rape, the list would be never ending. Men thought that it was okay to burn Women alive because they're upsetting a god they have never seen or met. Those book-bounded religions are peak closed mindedness that all untrained males have in them. Insecure and afraid minds trying to establish control.

The way a bunch from the 70 million extra men in India and China have been crying about men being oppressed is peak incompetence. You could not oppress or control the male in any form in the patriarchal age of Pisces. I am still wondering why after 2000 years of patriarchy, the "superior sex" still needs men's rights activist movements and for Feminists to care about their issues.

You had spiritual support, entire government systems were patriarchal, Women had no power, you were being worshipped, had the male-made "God" on your side – yet you still need men's rights activist movements today. And you find it offensive when I say that males are incapable of leadership. Facts do not care about your feelings. You are wired to hoard resources and be selfish, yet you failed at that too. Women still managed to overpower and intimidate you enough for you to feel the need of creating a men's rights activism collective to protect yourself after the support of the age of Pisces, masculine number 1, and the whole patriarchy on your side. Peak incompetence.

Oppressing men would not be possible in the age of Pisces. The low vibrations that took power over the planet supported the masculine energy over the Feminine. I am happy that they feel oppressed though. They are just

manifesting a Matriarchy for us by claiming that Women are privileged and that we live in a Gynocentric society.

Women are utterly powerful and men are utterly incompetent.

The masculine energy is evil. I do not like the term "divine masculine" because I'm yet to find anything divine about masculinity.

I also offer that the name of Feminism be changed. The name number of Feminism is 31 3+1 = 4. 4 is the number of struggles and hardships. Instead, we call this movement Phylogynism which comes at 4+1 = 5. 5 being the number of balance.

As we approach the ending of the book, there is one last topic that needs to be discussed.

VI
The Pick-Me

This chapter is dedicated to understanding the pick-me, the self-hating superior being, the mighty elephant tied to a shrub by a fragile rope. But before that, lets discuss the Bhartiya Naari or Indian Woman that India worships. The concept of a Bhartiya Naari is absurd but just so true to how men view everyone and everything who is not them.

Bhartiya Naari or Indian Woman is the embodiment of strength. The strength in question is not being a leader who is strong enough to bring positive changes to a society, no, it's a strong woman who can endure all pain, suffering, and discriminations that a male lead society subjects her to. She has strength, but in a way that a man would want her to have. The strength to stay with her husband after all the beatings and punches.

She's self-sacrificing. Need I describe this quality more? She cuts pieces off herself to feed others. The others in question being the male ego. She is the one who will sacrifice her individuality to serve a nuclear family, allegedly created and owned by the sperm dispenser of the family, that he apparently is the head of. The same guy who

sits quietly at the doctor's office while his wife talks to the Doctor about the pain in his prostate.

She is the embodiment of purity. Not a pure soul who holds no negative emotions such as grudges, hate, anger, envy, greed, or jealousy. No, she's someone who's never had a penis inside her vagina. The male view of the world is low, and us accepting their worldview brings us to their level.

A pick-me is basically just a woman who accepts the male world view. The one who believes that she is indeed created to serve a man. Not only that, she's also keeping other women in oppression under males. Fear of men creates a pick-me. No, not the pick-me feminist who unknowingly adds to the very patriarchy she claims to be against, this woman ensures her own survival by genuinely becoming the most loyal pet men have in order to get whipped the least. She will exist in public spaces among Women and men, but she will make sure the men know that she's on their side and how she's so cool because she's not like other Women.

She is adding to the patriarchy weather or not she decides to voice her misogynistic self-hating opinions or not. Women should always be view as extremely important. Women are far more important than men, especially when it comes to society. 'Ladies first' is a societal benefit. Women hating themselves along with hatred toward Matriarchal Women leads to the downfall of civilizations. The reason why the world is messed up is because women do not love themselves. It is not a conscious decision that Women trapped under patriarchal control make. It's not Women's fault as no one choses to self-harm. Right from their childhood, Women have been beaten, broken, and bullied into hating themselves because Women's self- hate leads to a patriarchy and Women's self-love leads to a Matriarchy

and hence a better society.

That's why the patriarchy has always aimed to make Women hate and underestimate themselves. Convincing them that they are inherently inferior and created for men to use, when in reality they are far above men, ensures that they do not center or prioritize themselves. Telling Women that the best way to exist as a Woman is by being a self-sacrificing punching bag, trains the female psyche into keeping herself last. Women can be the source of abundance or scarcity, her freedom, happiness, and centering herself brings fortune and blessings onto civilizations and families. Shaming the female sexuality leads to a collective sexual guilt and hence sexual crimes in society. How you treat women is how a country becomes. Thats why a country cannot progress more than its women. So, if a country is internationally humiliated with homelessness and poverty, with garbage on the street and crime everywhere, it is reflecting how they treat women.

A Female Supremacy and men's exploitation to empower Women is necessary. Your country is shit because you treat Women like shit.

You are a Woman. You're far more powerful and not dependent on men's treatment to have a good life. Your self-love is extremely powerful. As a Woman, you're constantly shooting out your own energy into others. Recently, on the Girlstagram, we saw a lot of conversations around decentering men. This was Women realizing that they had been brainwashed into centering relationships with men and prioritizing men in their lives. They began to see that they did not need to have a boyfriend or even to get married one day. They started to see how they're programmed to sacrifice their own happiness and needs in order to keep a man. It extends beyond just romantic relationships. Every

moment you spend believing that you're equal to, and not above men, you're indulging in self-hate. Your energy should and must be moving towards yourself constantly. You should be thinking about your needs, goals, and desires constantly, and I mean, literally thinking and focusing on you. Stop selling pieces of yourself to please others. Learning to be gentle, kind, and empathetic towards yourself is way more important than helping others for you. Do what you love, not what you've been taught to love. You do not have to share any cakes with men, the whole thing belongs to you. As the physical embodiments of the Mother Nature, the world belongs to you. The world IS for you. Gynocentricism is the order. You are the center of this world. So, act like it. If you love him, he will love himself. But if you love yourself, he will love you, and I'm not just talking about romantic relationships. Decenter men, learn about why they exist and treat them as that. You both are not equals, don't aim to be lower. He will give up his seat for you. It's the male sexuality that also must be controlled and constantly be prone to shaming.

If as a Woman, you do not prioritize and center directly and only yourself, then you will be used and exploited left and right.

Do you see how powerful you are? Just your mere shift of energy from him to yourself can move mountains for you. We often watch videos on YouTube regarding 'how to get in touch with our Feminine energy.' The Femininity coach often talks, but how you should do these activities and take care your yourself? What exactly is happening? Does bathing unlock your Feminine Matriarch energy? No, it's the time you spend focusing on yourself during those baths. Is it taking yourself on dates? No, it's the letting the universe know that you're treating yourself with something special from time to time. Is it the spas? No, it's the willingness to

spend time worshipping yourself. The real deal here is the energy and the attention. You do not have to spend money, just pay attention to yourself. Look at yourself and feel the existence of your holy body. That's centering your energy back to yourself.

Thats all you have to do to establish a Matriarchy. It's to love yourself and centering yourself.

A pick-me is actually just a Woman giving men easy access to her, her resources, and abilities, so that men don't whip her to extract them.

Bhartiya Naari is also compassionate. By definition, compassion means sympathetic pity and concern for the sufferings or misfortunes of others. Of others. You as a Woman are seen as a giver. Your consent does not matter and that's why rape is not taken seriously.

It's still not fair to hate pick-me Women. The society has put both Women and men through the same patriarchal brainwashing process. It would be unfair to put special pressure on Women to be feministic. I know that we all feel tempted to hate on pick-me Women, but no matter who a Woman chooses to be, she is still physically, biologically, emotionally, and spiritually superior to men, and still has the key to creating a Matriarchy within herself.

All women, unfortunately, even the most misogynistic pick-me, carries within herself the key to the Matriarchy, and since she's so powerful and can create a Matriarchy, she can also destroy it. Women's internalized misogyny leading to self-hate is keeping the patriarchy alive. In no way must you ever still blame a Woman because we all were subjected to both conscious and subconscious training to hate women. Be grateful that you made, at least consciously, your way out of it.

Women's subconscious desires are much more powerful than that of men. Women are creating the reality. Our deep inward desires create our reality. Which is why throughout the book I put an emphasis on how we all are governed by our subconscious minds, no matter who we consciously choose to be. A pick-me Woman is again, a reflection of what lies deep within our subconscious. You have the power to create the reality that you want, but first you must fix the production system. Remember that you are far more powerful than men, and you can move mountains. You have the power within yourself, you just have to figure out how to channel it properly.

One of the main reasons why Women hate non-feminist Women is because "how dare you support the one who oppresses you over your own side?! This is what makes our movement weak!" But the truth is that you do not need anyone's support to achieve your goals.

You, as a feminist or a Philogynist, do not require the support of Women. You do not need all Women to be feminists in order to find success in your endeavor as a Womanitarian. History shows that most Women have never been feminists. Study the history of Women, and you will discover that the few rights Women achieved were given to us by a minority of dedicated Women. The goal of feminism became to become palatable so that more Women would become feminists, and the result was disastrous. There will always be Women who fail to recognize their subconscious programming that the patriarchy fed them, and will always function in fear. If your goal as a feminist is to base yourself on the opinion of each Woman, then you will remain stagnant forever. Philogynism is the only political ideology that will defend Women as a class.

Feminism is not supposed to be the all accepting kind and loving movement of inclusion. Feminism is a movement only for women, which aims towards not only ending femicide, but also creating a Female-led society.

When a pickmeisha chooses to voice her anti-feminist opinions, she's still a feminist. The only way for a Woman to be an anti-feminist is by doing and being exactly what the patriarchy expects of her; to be a loyal slave to her master. If she's choosing to live her life the way she desires, she is still a feminist. The only way to be a misogynistic Woman is by being under a man's control.

Even a hateful pick-me Women only harms herself and other Women. She is not the enemy because she is not the one gaining from this. She is not exchanging other Women's lives for her own luxury, even if she might think so. Every time she harms another Women, she is unconsciously harming herself and strengthening the male control over herself as well as others.

Women are never the enemy. The enemy is the class that benefits from your suffering and self-hate. The enemy in the case of a patriarchy is the males.

In conclusion, your entire existence, needs, problems, desires, role, and values are hated. I am guessing as someone who's every thought is hated, you already realize this. But what does a woman do with this realization? She internalizes it. Most Women will end up internalizing this rejection as self-hate. Compassion towards women is the key to unlocking a Matriarchy. Love for Women and hatred of men need to always come together. In fact, if you love Women, then you must hate males, because how can you not hate the sex class who have been torturing Women for centuries like this, if you truly love Women?